A Wife's Guide to Baseball

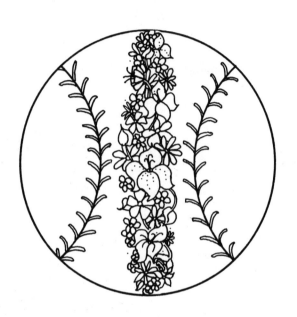

A Wife's Guide to Baseball

❧

By Charline Gibson and Michael Rich

With Notes from the Mound by Bob Gibson

And a Foreword by Mrs. Bowie Kuhn

NEW YORK / THE VIKING PRESS

To the memory of Johnny Keane, who enriched not only baseball by his wisdom and understanding, but the lives of all those who were privileged to know him.

Copyright © 1970 by Charline Gibson and
Michael B. Rich
All rights reserved
First published in 1970 by The Viking Press, Inc.
625 Madison Avenue, New York, N.Y. 10022
Published simultaneously in Canada by
The Macmillan Company of Canada Limited
SBN 670-76585-6
Library of Congress catalog card number: 77-115096
Printed in U.S.A.

Foreword

by Mrs. Bowie Kuhn

I grew up at a time when baseball was essentially a man's game—that is, male fans felt that the game was exclusively *theirs*, not just to play, as a few of them might have done, but to reminisce and recriminate about while resurrecting great days and great plays of bygone years.

Although distaff enthusiasm for baseball was not specifically discouraged, any girl who expressed an incipient interest was likely to find her questions answered, if at all, with impatient tolerance. Not surprisingly, girls soon tired of this heavy-handed, slightly hostile male attitude and, for many, the impulse to follow baseball died aborning.

As everyone knows, the sociology of American life underwent enormous changes in the period following World War II. During the war thousands of women served in armed-forces auxiliaries, and millions took jobs in defense plants. In so doing, they not only freed men for active duty but also gained a certain measure of personal and financial independence for themselves, and a measure of self-confidence in their new-found equality. Whether equality between the sexes is good or not is one of the very few questions about which most men will argue even more heatedly than about baseball itself. In any case, one way in which women of my emancipated era exhibited their independence was with a renewed interest in sports.

Today, more women than ever before like baseball. Even so, only a small percentage of them perceive the many levels on which baseball can be appreciated: as highly charged emotional drama, as an athletic ballet, as a fiercely contested struggle between managerial strategists, to name but a few.

One reason for this is that baseball has a paradoxical character. It seems almost simplistic: you hit the ball and run. Right?

Wrong. The game is built upon a store of fundamental tactics and techniques. It is the players' skills which make the supremely difficult appear easy. Also, much of baseball's fascination lies not only in *what* is happening, but in *why*—the choices before a manager, as well, of course, as how successfully the manager's players carry out his strategy. Thus, the baseball fan-to-be must be armed with some understanding of the game. It is to that noble goal that this book is addressed.

How does a woman become a baseball fan? My own career as a devotee of the game is only slightly atypical. As a youngster living in Philadelphia, I rooted passionately for the A's. My husband was a baseball fan long before he became a lawyer. As Commissioner, he is no less a fan. I must confess that my interest has taken on a new dimension as a result of my husband's career. I have been able to meet and talk with players whom I would otherwise know only from headlines and dreams.

You may suspect a certain "official" intensity to my interest in baseball. Not at all. There is a fascination to the game that I find unduplicated elsewhere in the world of sports. Not the least of this appeal is that baseball is a family affair. It is something of a cliché, but yet quite true, that there are increasingly few things that Americans can enjoy together as families. Baseball is certainly one. Our four children range in age from eight to seventeen. We have usually gone to games *en masse*, so I can say something of the relaxed mutuality of a family's being able to talk about an experience in which every member has shared. I can't recall a single game our family attended that we didn't enjoy. Each of us roots independently— that is, for his or her favorite team—except the head of the family, who impartially (and silently) hopes for a tie. But if my husband may not root for one particular team, the rest of us suffer from no such inhibitions. In company with fans everywhere, the more vocal part of the family leaves the ball park cheerful or despondent, the conversation either a triumphant recapitulation or a grieving autopsy.

Baseball is more than a game. It is part of America's history and your heritage. Baseball has enriched our language and given our folklore yesterday's heroes—and tomorrow's. Beyond all else, baseball is an intense game of talent and temper, desire and frustration. Baseball is the inevitable certainty that keeps you tense in your seat or brings you cheering to your feet. Baseball is the tangy aroma of hot dogs and the crackle of peanuts shelled by nervous fingers. Baseball is the kids who watch their heroes with awe and wonderment and who, even if the game is lost, still yell their encouragement. Baseball is young lovers who hold hands while cheering a spectacular play, and the moods of joy or gloom which sweep over the crowd as the score changes. Baseball is . . .

For a woman, baseball is a game to see and be seen at. And the season is now.

Contents

ACKNOWLEDGMENTS

I am indebted to Cal Hubbard, Supervisor of Umpires for the American League, for reading those sections of the manuscript devoted to the umpire—and for not ejecting me from the game. I am grateful to Monte Irvin of the Office of the Commissioner for his wise comments about hitting. Jack Buck provided insights into the sportscaster's behind-the-microphone view of baseball.

Many people said, when they heard I was working on this book, "Oh, what a good idea." And though they remain anonymous, their reaction helped give me the courage to persevere, though they can hardly be held responsible for the literary consequences. I must give special thanks to Elinor Upton, Ethel Rosenberg, and Priscilla Glenn, who shared the labors of first deciphering and then retyping the original manuscript I provided. And to Pat O'Brien, who was indefatigable in his search for answers to my endless questions.

And I certainly thank my husband, who appended his comments to the manuscript with care and tolerance. Finally, I am grateful to Red Schoendienst, the manager of the St. Louis Cardinals, who allowed the questions about baseball on behalf of this book to infiltrate his clubhouse and, through it all, kept my husband in his pitching rotation.

Introduction

"Play ball."

The umpire's imperative launches the major-league baseball season—by tradition, with games in Cincinnati and Washington on the first Monday in April. But for weeks before, the approach of the season is heralded in homes across the nation.

Equipment is freed from winter-long storage in closet and attic. Gloves are oiled, bats hefted with enthusiasm born of winter's long confinement— occasionally with tragic results for a favorite lamp. At dinner, Dad and the kids heatedly debate how their favorite teams will do in this year's pennant race. Often the talk is in alphabetical code—ERAs and RBIs—or equally mysterious phrases: "He can't go to his right," or, "They're weak in the bull-pen."

Like a virus, a strange and wonderful mania

spreads throughout the nation. This is the American rite of spring.

The fan's passionate devotion is not likely to abate in the months ahead. True, his team cannot win all its games, and may lose many more than it wins. But his loyalty remains undiminished, for always there is the game tomorrow, and tomorrow —and then perhaps a rueful wait till next year.

During the season, a fan views his team's ball park as a shrine. His attendance at as many games possible is a semi-religious observance that has its own litany of cheers or boos. When a fan cannot be at the game in person, he is there in spirit. The transistor radio's play-by-play broadcasts are his companions on the golf course, at the seashore, in the back yard. The family television set stays stubbornly tuned to whatever channel carries the games of the Team.

But if the baseball season is a time of special satisfaction for the American male, it is all too often his wife's season of discontent. True, more and more wives have come to realize that baseball is not exclusively *his* game but theirs too. But for most, the cry of "Play ball" still ushers in a time of confusion and dwindling patience. Suppers are delayed by extra innings, and weekend afternoons are empty because Dad and Junior have disappeared to observe the Mystery of the Game at first hand. You spend fretful evenings trying to read while the sportscaster's voice rises in a crescendo of joyful excitement, and the Fan excitedly enters the room with a gleeful "Hit a hanging curve to the opposite field and cleared the sacks." Even if you don't understand, you'd better look as pleased as he is, and woe to you if you fail to appreciate the importance of what has just taken place.

Baseball is a game for everyone. However, in common with most things in life, your enjoyment of the game is in direct proportion to your understanding of it. Certainly you may be indifferently aware that a player is out after three strikes, and perhaps yawningly conscious that a home run is cause for joy—or deep gloom, if hit by the opposition. But these are simply scattered pieces of intelligence.

You can enjoy baseball simply as a contest between two teams. Better still, you can watch it with an understanding of what makes a great play sharply different from a routine one—though even the routine one is far from easy. Best of all, you can see baseball as a kaleidoscope of action and drama in which two managers try to outguess and outthink each other while their respective teams try to outplay each other. And you will have a lot of fun. Baseball can be a family affair. And wouldn't it be nice, just once, when your husband explodes with indignation over an "out" call at second base, to smile sweetly and say, "But dear, he had to tag him because the force was off." Mind you, just once. Or twice.

Since no wife can expect to be entirely free from the baseball expertise of her husband, *my* husband has offered occasional comments and observations on this book, which appear as footnotes. And since he is a major-league pitcher, you can use his professional opinions to reinforce your position during the inevitable (friendly) arguments that you'll have with your own husband.

How much do you know about baseball? The wide variety of answers that readers may give to that question—from "Nothing" to "More than the manager of the team I root for"—poses a special quandary for the author. After all, I don't want to belabor you with needless explanations. On the other hand, I don't want to leave you floundering in search of the definition for a fairly routine term.

I think I have resolved this dilemma to the satisfaction of both the beginning and the more advanced fan. I assume that the readers of this volume do know the significant difference between a ball and a strike; and that they know that baseball is played in nine units called innings, in which first one team and then the other bats until three outs have been recorded, at which time the team that was in the field comes to bat and the team that was at bat goes on defense, taking the field. I also assume that you know what a fly ball is and what a ground ball is, and I shall try not to assume much more than that.

Should even these assumptions about your baseball education prove unfounded, fear not. At the back of this book is what I hope will prove to be a most useful feature: a glossary of baseball terms. Unlike the usual glossary, this one is not placed there merely to add extra pages to the book, nor is it intended to be read only after you finish the rest of this book. I hope it can be an illuminating companion as you read. If something in the text puzzles you, check with the glossary for a fuller explanation. If you fail to find the answer there, I refer you to that irrefutable source of all knowledge, located right in your household: your husband.

A Wife's Guide to Baseball

The Field

Home Base shall be marked by a five-sided slab of whitened rubber. It shall be a 12-inch square with two of the corners filled in so that one edge is 17 inches long, two are 8½ inches and two are 12 inches. It shall be set in the ground with the point at the intersection of the lines extending from home base to first base and to third base; with the 17-inch edge facing the pitcher's plate, and the two 12-inch edges coinciding with the first and third base lines. The top edges of home base shall be beveled and the base shall be fixed in the ground level with the ground surface.—*Official Baseball Rules*

Your first glimpse of a major-league baseball field might suggest a contemporary pastoral scene. A carefully manicured "lawn" stretches to the limits of the field, interrupted by a nonobjective arrangement of bare earth. A disciplined pattern of white lines, circles, and squares contrasts pleasingly with the rich green grass.

There is, of course, nothing bucolic about this setting. Nor is the field decorated at random with geometric figures. It is a stage, drawn to exacting specifications, for a drama of often epic proportions.

Home base, which is described at the beginning of this chapter in the stiff, formal prose of the

Baseball Rules Committee, is the prime point of baseball's four-carat diamond.* Diagram No. 1 shows this clearly. If you stand on home, first base is 90 feet away to your right; directly ahead of you is second base, just over 127 feet away from home, and 90 feet from first; third base is on your left, 90 feet from second, and 90 feet from home. The whole diamond-patterned area is called "the infield."

Now, imagine you are standing at home, looking straight ahead toward second base. Sixty feet and six inches away is a hump of dirt, a mound which at its top is 10 inches higher than the rest of the infield. This is the pitcher's mound, or "the hill." Atop it and half buried in the soil is a slab of whitened rubber 24 inches long and 6 inches wide. This is the "pitcher's plate," according to the rulebook.**

Still imagining yourself at home plate, notice that a white line runs from home to first base and *beyond*, continuing in a straight line until it meets a wall or, perhaps, part of the grandstand. This is the right-field foul line. A similar line extends from the plate to third base and beyond. This is the left-field foul line. These two foul lines, like a giant V balanced on the plate, distinguish "fair" ground from "foul." Inside the V—that is, to the left of the right-field line, to the right of the left-field line—is *fair* territory. Everything to the right

---

* My wife is technically correct in her reference to "home base." But neither players nor fans are so formal. It is "home," or "the plate," or, rarely, "home plate," but *never* "home base."

** Here again, the jargon of the game has supplanted the official verbiage. The "pitcher's plate" is always referred to as "the rubber."

of the right-field line and to the left of the left-field line is *foul*.

Mark this well, for grasping the distinction between fair and foul ground is essential to understanding what is happening on the field. If you have listened, even with only one ear, to a sportscaster's description of a game, you have probably heard the expression "Baseball is a game of inches." And so it is. More often than not, the critical inches are those which determine whether the point at which a ball falls to earth is fair or foul.

Let's continue our careful appraisal of the field. If you look at the ground immediately around home—or glance at Diagram No. 1—you will notice several chalked geometric figures. Flanking the plate are two rectangles measuring 6 feet long by 4 feet wide. These are the batters' boxes. Linked to them, and directly behind the plate, is an open rectangle of similar proportions, the catcher's box. (If you are wondering whether someone has to painstakingly measure the required dimensions to work out the boxes before each game, you will be relieved to know that a template of constant dimensions is used as a guide—much as you might use a cooky cutter in the kitchen.)*

Behind and to each side of the plate are two circles which are officially called "next batter's box." Nonetheless, they are circles. Otherwise, they are accurately named, providing an authorized location for the player who will follow his teammate to the plate. While he waits in the circle he is "on deck" or "in the on-deck circle."

As you might suspect by now, baseball has a large and rich vocabulary all its own. To avoid

* The choice of analogy is entirely my wife's.

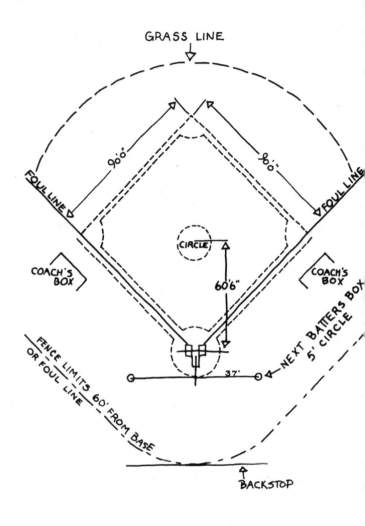

GRASS LINE

90'0"

90'0"

FOUL LINE

FOUL LINE

CIRCLE

COACH'S BOX

COACH'S BOX

60'6"

NEXT BATTERS BOX 5' CIRCLE

FENCE LIMITS 60' FROM BASE
OR FOUL LINE

37'

BACKSTOP

Diagram No. 1

confusing you (further?) I will always attempt to explain the "officialese" term and then indicate the equivalent expression in the argot of the game. Once I have given the definition, only the contemporary language of the sport will be used. Thus, in these pages at least, "next batter's box" has been forever replaced by "on-deck circle." This, I hope, will help you to become an articulate fan as well as a knowledgeable one.

Our survey of the area around the plate is now complete, so let's take a stroll around the bases.

Walking toward first base from home is a little like driving on a narrow dirt road that is (improbably) divided by a white line. The basepath (the road) is 6 feet wide. It is bisected by the right-field foul line, so that half the basepath is in fair ground and half in foul. For exactly half the way to first—45 feet—the 3-foot width of the basepath in foul ground is marked by another white line parallel to the foul line, thus forming a skinny lane. This three-foot-wide area—the rules, somewhat mysteriously, call it "the three-foot lane"—is the approach lane for a batter to use when running to first. We'll return to the "three-foot lane" in the chapter on umpiring.

We now arrive at first base, a white canvas bag securely fastened to the ground. The base is 15 inches square, at least 3 inches—but not more than 5 inches—thick. Note that the entire bag is inside the foul line, that is, to the foul line's left, and therefore is in fair ground. If you kick the bag, you'll find it firm but resilient. In foul territory, 15 feet to the right of the line, is a white-lined rectangle, the first-base coach's box.

Let's wander toward second base. There are no chalked lines to guide us and, away from the loom of the stands, there is a feeling of spaciousness. But the distance from first to second is the same—90 feet—that separates all the bases from one another.

The area between second and third is, like that between second and first, an expanse of smooth bare earth sandwiched between the infield and outfield grass. Third base is, like second and first, securely fastened to the ground. The bag abuts the left-field foul line, just as first abuts the right-field line. The third-base coach's box is in foul ground 15 feet to the left of the line.

As you walk toward home you may feel a peculiar sense of exhilaration, and when you get to the plate, instead of stepping over it or just putting one foot on it, you may want to jump on it with both feet. Perhaps it is a childish feeling, but it's one I always have—and surrender to—on my infrequent excursions across the diamond.

Standing on the field in a major-league ball park is guaranteed to make you feel tiny. The empty stands seem to tower threateningly over the infield, and the outfield is like a huge grassy prairie. This heightened sense of space and distance is especially true of modern ball parks, and with good reason. A baseball rule provides that any major-league playing field constructed after June 1, 1958, shall measure 325 feet down the right- and left-field foul lines, and at least 400 feet to the center-field fence. These are minimum distances, and a number of modern ball parks exceed one or more of the specified dimensions. Older ball parks (those built before 1950) often feature highly individual field configurations. This variance in the size of the outfield—the infield is always the same size—is significant for several reasons.

A team plays exactly half of its games at home. As you might expect, if the home team's park had fences that were out of reach of all but the mightiest hitters, that team would emphasize defense. It would try to have good pitching and fast outfielders to patrol the large outfield area.

If the home team had several right-handed sluggers, the left-field fence might be much closer to the plate than the fences in center or right.* If the team was weak at bat but saddled with a small park, it might "adjust" this situation by building wire fences atop the concrete or wooden outfield fences already in place—assuming that there was no room to push the fences back. As you can see, the dimensions of a ball park can have a profound effect on the offensive and defensive character of the team that plays there.

Back in the days when the Dodgers belonged to Brooklyn, the right fielder was Carl Furillo, dubbed the Reading Rifle in recognition of his Pennsylvania home and powerful arm. The right-field wall in tiny Ebbets Field was just 297 feet from home plate. In addition, the wall was topped by a wire screen. Within this shortened right field, and in front of a high wall, Furillo could play unreasonably shallow (close to the infield) against all but the strongest left-handed hitters. This situation, combined with his strong arm, frequently enabled him to throw a runner out at first base on what would have been a line drive single in almost any other ball park. Not surprisingly, Furillo led the National League in outfield "assists"—throws

* The power of a hitter is usually to the same side of the field as the side of *the plate* he bats from. Right-handed hitters generally have their power to left field, lefties to right field.

resulting in a runner being put out—in 1950 and 1951.*

The present stabilized dimensions for ball parks have had another effect. Bigger ball parks tend to be pitchers' parks, simply because the more room there is, the harder it is for a hitter to swat the ball over the fence. Also, the fly ball that might have hit an outfield wall and gone for a double or a triple is now just a long out.

Mentioning the outfield wall reminds me that I have neglected to discuss two other features of a baseball field. The first is quite literally on the field—the "outfield track." About 20 feet in front of the outfield walls, the grass ends and the ground is bare. This is to protect the outfielder, who might otherwise run full tilt into the wall. For with his back to the plate and his eyes fixed on a hitter's drive, the outfielder cannot judge his nearness to the wall without taking his eyes off the flight of the ball. But he can *listen* for it. As soon as he crosses from outfield grass to outfield track he will hear the difference in the sound of his running steps—a sure warning that he is approaching the wall. In some ball parks the ground immediately in

* As a rule, a team will assign the outfielder with the strongest throwing arm to right field. Positioned there, a strong and accurate arm—the players call it a "rifle" or a "cannon"—can perform two important defensive tasks. First, it tends to discourage base runners from taking the "extra base"—meaning that a runner on first will think twice about trying to go to third when his teammate hits a single to right. It also tends to inhibit "stretching"—trying to make a double out of a single, or a triple out of a double. And—well, perhaps we'd better wait for the lady to finish the preliminary explanations before we discuss anything too esoteric.

front of the fences slopes sharply upward, also signaling the nearness of the wall. For additional protection, several clubs have affixed strips of foam rubber to the outfield fences—a kind of bumper to protect the players, not the fences.

My other omission isn't on the field, at least never on the playing surface of the field. The "bull-pen" is the area where relief pitchers warm up before coming into the game. The bullpen is off the playing field, either in foul ground down the left- or right-field line, or hidden beyond the out-field walls and only partly visible from the stands. For obvious reasons, the visiting team's bullpen is separate from that of the home team. Why is it called the bullpen? Nobody seems to know for sure. There are two frequent explanations. One is that in the tradition-shrouded beginnings of baseball pitchers awaiting a summons to the mound whiled away their time by chewing tobacco, the favorite brand being Bull Durham. The other is that, with time on their hands, the players do little else but sling the bull.

Up till now I have described only open stadiums —ones without a full roof. As just about everybody knows, there is one completely covered stadium already in use, and more are contemplated. The Houston Astrodome is a marvel of engineering, measuring 218 feet from the playing field to the highest point of its soaring dome. Foul-line dimensions are 328 feet down the left-field line, 406 feet to straightaway center, and 366 feet down the right-field line. One of the benefits of playing in the Astrodome is that it is air-conditioned—a virtual necessity for daytime baseball in Texas.

The Astrodome is unquestionably impressive, both inside and out. Some ballplayers like playing in it; others don't, complaining that the ball doesn't "carry" well for the hitters and that a fly ball can be difficult to judge against the dome's painted roof panels. Of course, the less than total satisfaction of some visiting ballplayers may be precisely because they are a visiting ball club and play only a few games in the Astrodome. Certainly the Houston Astro players seem to like it. But, I admit, I don't. There is something unreal, at least to me, about watching a baseball game *inside*. I like to sit in the stands and feel the warmth of the sun rather than hear the whine of the air conditioners. My prejudice aside, if you get to Houston you will be missing a fascinating experience if you don't go to the Astrodome.

One feature of the Astrodome that is being reflected elsewhere is the use of Astroturf instead of grass. Astroturf is a synthetic material made by Monsanto Chemical Company which, it is claimed, feels as if it were grass underfoot. Moreover, it can withstand the weather a lot better than grass can. And there's no chance of a player catching his spikes in a hole, as he might on a grass field, since Astroturf is completely smooth. In Houston, Astroturf covers both the infield and the outfield. It has been installed by the Chicago White Sox on the infield in White Sox Park and is under consideration for other ball parks.

If you are thinking of replacing your lawn with Astroturf, think again. The installation at White Sox Park cost more than $100,000, just for the infield. But caring for ball-park grass is no snap, either. It's a job for professionals: the groundskeepers. Every (grass) park has a full crew of these professionals, who plant, water, resod, and replace the divots torn by the players' spikes. If you are a slave to a lawn of your own, you can easily imagine the task of maintaining several acres of grass constantly abused by steel-shod athletes. The dirt sections of the infield are rolled, screened— to get rid of even the tiniest stones, which can cause a ground ball to take an erratic bounce— and watered to keep the dust down. The preferred grasses change somewhat according to geography. For example, Merion blue in the East (Shea Stadium and Yankee Stadium); a mixture of Merion, Prado, and Kentucky Blue at Dodger Stadium in Los Angeles.

Grass can even play a tactical role in a ball game. For example, if your team's infielders are a little slow, you can instruct your groundskeepers to keep the grass tall, thus effectively slowing down ground balls and perhaps enabling your infielders to throw out runners who might otherwise beat out an infield hit. On the other hand, if your team is reasonably fast and can handle a bat, you may water your infield hardly at all. The resulting dry, hard surface will send normal ground balls ricocheting off its unyielding surface, particularly if your hitters make a point of hammering down on the ball.

If during a game already in progress it should begin to rain hard enough to interfere with play, the umpires will signal the ground crew to cover the infield with a "tarp." This is a great big rubber or plastic sheet—actually several sheets—usually mounted on an enormous roller. The ground crew's task is to get the field covered as quickly as possible, lest the downpour of a summer shower turn the field into a quagmire. Ground crews from different teams "compete" with each other to see who can cover the infield in the least time. (If you have occasion to send your husband out to cover the lawn furniture, you might use a similar stratagem, based on neighborhood competition, to spur him on.)

So much for the physical environment in which the game of baseball is played. If your husband is also reading this book he may deprecatingly suggest that this chapter is incomplete. And he'll be right, in the sense that almost any aspect of baseball provides unlimited fuel for arguments, based on a hundred years of baseball history and the passionate prejudices of its fans. I have tried to summarize the topography of baseball, at ground level. But nature can take a higher hand.

To paraphrase Mark Twain, everybody may want the game to begin, but nobody can turn off the rain. Or turn up the thermostat to banish the chilling cold of early spring.* If the wind is blowing "in" (that is, toward home) it will help the pitchers by keeping aloft fly balls that might otherwise drop for hits, and by keeping in play a ball that might otherwise go for a homer. Of course, if the wind is blowing out, it will generally help the hitters.** Even the shadows cast by the grandstand

---

* Except in a domed stadium, where the weather is controlled by man, not nature.
** One of the classic examples of "wind damage" occurred during the 1961 All-Star game, played at San Francisco's Candlestick Park, which is famous (or infamous) for its high-velocity air currents. Stu Miller, the slightly built pitcher for the National League, was literally blown off the mound, committing a "balk." A balk occurs when a pitcher, with one foot on the rubber, starts to throw toward the plate or any base and fails to complete that throw. The rulebook, written before Candlestick Park was built, makes no pro-

in the late-afternoon sun can help or hurt. A pitcher throwing from a mound in the sun enjoys advantage when the ball suddenly enters a shadowed area around the plate, because the hitter has more difficulty in following the flight of the ball.

Major-league baseball games have been held up by more than weather; spectators, dogs, cats have appeared on the diamond. Swallows and pigeons stubbornly circling home have driven umpires and players into a rage. And in one case—in Ebbets Field, of course—a game was called because of gnats swarming round the Dodgers in the infield like a plague cast by the visiting team.

Every field has two dugouts, one along the first-base side, the other on the third-base side of the field. The dugouts are roofed—and in some cases air-conditioned—and feature a long bench to accommodate the team, a water-cooler, and a bat rack which holds the "lumber." The water-cooler has a rather interesting role. In addition to furnishing the players with liquid refreshment, it is also the scapegoat for a player's or manager's temper, enduring countless kicks and curses when things are going less than well. Under less violent circumstances, it is the destination of a merely restless manager, who paces nervously between the cooler and his seat on the bench.

In most parks a tunnel from the dugout leads under the stands to the clubhouse. The clubhouse includes the manager's office, the equipment room where bats and the trunks that carry the team's equipment on the road are stored, the locker room, and the trainer's room. The locker room includes

---

vision for local weather conditions. A wind-blown balk is still a balk.

a locker for each man, and an annex with showers. The trainer's quarters boasts an impressive inventory of equipment—tables on which athletes can receive massages, whirlpool and diathermy equipment for relaxing strained muscles, and a "medicine cabinet" peculiar to the needs of athletes.*

One more point before we get to the individual players and their positions.

A baseball team can be either more or less than the sum of the talent its players possess. A team which is, man for man, inferior to others can sometimes—by its belief in itself, its overwhelming desire to come out on top, its pride and determination—raise itself beyond reasonable expectations and discover destiny. In baseball, such qualities are summed up in a single word: hustle.

Hustle is doing everything to the best of your ability. Hustle is conquering your fatigue or momentary disappointment. Hustle is not giving up on any play, or on your future or your team's. Hustle is trying, trying—and trying yet again.

Nothing speaks more eloquently of the role of psychology in baseball than the striving of all managers to instill in their players a sense of desire,

* The trainer plays a vital but unpublicized role. He must be able to minister to a host of injuries that players admit to, as well as being a good enough psychologist to know which players will try to hide an injury from him. Pitchers, for obvious reasons, are prone to arm trouble. Catchers—with equal obviousness—are likely to get split fingers from foul tips. Some players get "strawberries," reddish bruises on their thighs and hips, from sliding; others have a history of ankle injuries and require taping before every game. A good trainer can't win any games for a team, but he can prevent some losses by keeping the players in the best possible condition and by spotting an injury quickly and taking action to prevent it from getting worse.

both as individuals and as members of a team. This is a crucial point, for though twenty-five players may wear the same uniform, they will certainly differ markedly in their backgrounds, their tastes in everything from food to art, their politics, their attitudes toward life, their prejudices, and, of course, their professional ability.

They also differ as to race.

There is a disproportionate number of black ballplayers on every team. That is to say, there are more black athletes playing baseball than there should be, proportionate to the number of black Americans. Approximately one out of every ten Americans is black, but you will find far more than two black players on every baseball team. Why?

The best answer is that sports have offered a quick and effective way to escape the ghetto. Not only is there the opportunity to make a good salary, and the relative munificence of a darn good pension plan, but through athletics the individual black American acquires a positive identity. No longer, in Ralph Ellison's words, is he the invisible man. I am not suggesting that a black ballplayer is necessarily more egocentric than his white teammate, but simply that the newspaper stories about him—indeed, the actuality of seeing his name in print and of having people recognize his name and perhaps respond favorably to it—reaffirm his faith in himself. This is also true, I suppose, of many white ballplayers, but as a generalization I think it applies more fully and with greater intensity to blacks.

At this point I think I should state that nothing that I say here—or, for that matter, anywhere else in this book—necessarily applies to any member of the St. Louis Cardinals or their organization.

That such a disclaimer is necessary—or that I think it is necessary, which is much the same thing—is perhaps the best evidence of the role that race plays in baseball.

Race became an issue in baseball in 1947 when Jackie Robinson became the first black man to put on a major-league uniform. His success as a player and as a representative of his race was due to his own considerable talents and self-discipline, and to the good wishes and helpful efforts of many baseball people, all of whom were white. One in particular became a legend in his own time, and would have whether or not he had anything to do with black players in baseball: Mr. Branch Rickey. When I met him a few years ago he was a very old man, but his eyes still burned with a keen awareness of everything that was happening around him. He was a wise man and a wise baseball man, the kind of man one imagines always being called Mr. Rickey, regardless of his age. At any rate, before 1947 race was not an issue simply because there were no black ballplayers in the majors.

Progress in any area always seems woefully slow and inadequate when one looks backward. How easy everything seems to have been, and therefore how slow the progress. Of course this is an illusion fostered by history and the human personality, which prefers to recognize no time other than now. But Jackie Robinson had an exceedingly rough time. There were in those days players who refused to play with a black man and asked to be traded. Since then, things have improved tremendously. There are no segregated hotels or restaurants patronized by the major leagues, and black and white ballplayers can eat and sleep under the same roof—even in the same room.

Ah, you say, there is a trace of bitterness there; perhaps she feels sorry for herself. And, you continue, if black ballplayers are able to play, and they are doing better than they otherwise would be able to, why all the fuss?

I *am* slightly disappointed, rather than bitter. It does gall me (somewhat) that newspapers should carry headline stories about black and white ballplayers rooming together on the road. So what?

Part of the "what" is this. The great weight of tradition that baseball carries—its history, its heroes, the sameness of the game that makes comparisons of the game today and twenty years ago at least possible, if not completely accurate— is a burden as well as a mark of distinction. Baseball changes slowly. That is the secret of its continuing fascination for generations of Americans, and it is also the source of my dissatisfaction. I am not suggesting that black ballplayers *must* room with white ballplayers. But I would welcome an atmosphere in which such accommodations were possible without the publicity, which suggests that something strange is happening.

Baseball is highly contradictory. A white third baseman never hesitates before throwing to a black first baseman. It is only when the uniforms come off that race ever becomes an issue. Partly, it is an issue today because black ballplayers love the game every bit as much as white ballplayers do, but, unlike whites, they have no opportunity to manage in the major leagues or to have a significant front-office job or something similar. There are some black ballplayers who are eminently qualified for such positions, yet there has never been any suggestion that when their playing careers were over they would be able to continue to work within and for the game they love.

As individuals, blacks and whites get along well in baseball. That isn't to say that all ballplayers like each other. One is, after all, entitled to think that someone is arrogant or stupid or egotistical, so long as the opinion is held without regard to race, creed, religion, or country of national origin. Perhaps by the time you read this page a black manager will have been appointed in the major leagues, or a black front-office executive will have been hired. I hope so, for that will mean that another bar is down. Baseball has been good to the Gibsons, and we love the game, not for what it has done for us but for what it is. And when you love something you hate to discover an imperfection, particularly when it could be so easily removed.

But now we must leave the field, for according to the rules no spectators are permitted on the field during play. And the game is about to begin.

The Defense

The objective of each team is to win by scoring more runs than the opponent.—*Official Baseball Rules*

The corollary of the official objective is, of course, to prevent the other team from scoring as many runs as your team—and, if possible, to prevent them from scoring at all.

"Defense" is a somewhat broader term than most baseball fans would apply to this chapter. To many fans, fielding is what defense is all about. I have always thought the term curiously incomplete. True, fielding—the ability to move in front of a ground ball or catch up to a fly ball—is the basis of defense. But getting the glove on the ball is simply the last and most visible act in a defensive sequence. As we shall see, the individual effort of a fielder is largely dependent upon his natural gifts —his reflexes, his speed, and his ability to "get a good jump on the ball," to assess the direction and velocity of a long fly or a deep drive to the outfield at the instant the ball leaves the bat. But equally important is where the players are positioned on the field. It is no accident that the outfield is "around to right" when one left-handed hitter is up, and "straight away" when another left-handed hitter is up. But before we deal with the esoterics of baseball defense let's take a quick look at who plays where and what the general responsibilities of each player are.

The Battery

The pitcher and the catcher are called "the battery."* The pitcher has become the dominant figure in baseball.** His skills, or the lack of them, are, more than anything else, what win or lose ball games. The very fact that he and the catcher handle the ball more than any other player, underlines his crucial role. We will explore both these positions more fully in succeeding chapters. The battery is a team's first line of defense. For it is the avowed goal of the pitcher to strike out every opposing hitter. Assuming he doesn't manage to do this—and, of course, no pitcher has yet— he looks to his team's next line of defense: the infield.

The Infield

Four players man the bases: the first baseman, the second baseman, the third baseman, and the shortstop.

1. THE FIRST BASEMAN

The first baseman anchors the infield. After the pitcher and catcher, it is he who handles the ball most frequently. He is the recipient (one hesitates to say target) of a majority of the throws from the other infielders. Since infielders are as human

* The origin of the term is lost in the distant past, but it was used as early as 1886 in a noble work entitled *The Art of Pitching*.
** That's very touching. But would my wife say that if, for example, her husband was a shortstop?

as anyone else, not every throw to first is perfect, so the first baseman must be skilled at digging balls out of the dirt. In addition to such low throws in the dirt, other errant tosses may be to the right or left of the bag, requiring the first baseman to stretch—literally, to extend himself in a classic ballet split.

As a matter first of training and then of habit, a first baseman will extend his gloved hand as far as possible in the direction of the infielder throwing to first. This cuts down the time between the moment the ball is fielded and its arrival at first base. True, the difference is a fraction of a second, but that difference can be important on a close play at first. For example, assume that the batter has hit a slow ground ball to the shortstop, who races in and, in one smooth motion, sidearms the ball to first. The batter, of course, has not paused to admire the shortstop's artistry but has been tearing down the baseline in an attempt to beat the throw and thus, having touched first base before the ball arrives, be declared safe.

The first-base umpire would have to have two heads to determine visually which arrived at first base earlier, the batter or the infielder's throw. On such close plays at first, the umpire will watch the runner's feet and *listen* for the sound of the ball thudding into the first baseman's glove. If the runner's foot touches the bag before the umpire hears the thud, the runner is safe. If the throw's arrival is audible before the runner's foot hits the bag, the call is "Out."* On such a "bang-bang"

---

* For obvious reasons umpires call this a "look-and-listen play." It is well calculated to start an argument, no matter what the umpire calls.

play, the first baseman's stretch can make the difference.

In general, the first baseman will play off the bag, that is, somewhat toward second base and behind first base. However, with a strong left-handed hitter up, the first baseman will play closer to the bag. This is referred to as "guarding the line" and is another example of baseball's beloved tactical philosophy of playing the percentages. In this instance, there is a higher probability of a left-handed hitter hitting to the right side of the diamond, so the entire infield swings around to the right.

If there is a runner on first base, the first baseman may hold against the runner, which simply means that he will delay moving off the bag until the pitcher actually throws to the plate, for the pitcher may throw to first base in an attempt to pick off the runner.

With a runner on first and a right-handed hitter up, the first baseman may hold the runner on or ignore him. In this instance, the infield will normally be swung around to the left, and the manager may decree that in a particular situation it is better to provide maximum defensive coverage than to curtail the runner's lead.*

*A lead is the number of steps away from the base— first, second, or third—that a runner takes before the ball is pitched. The runner's lead is important for two reasons: first, because a long lead makes the execution of a double play more difficult; second, because a long lead encourages the runner to try to "steal." This particular form of baseball thievery simply means that a runner moves from one base to another on his own, without advancing as the result of any action by the hitter. Undoubtedly the best base-stealer in baseball is Lou Brock. Happily, he is a teammate of

2. THE SECOND BASEMAN

The second baseman shares the defensive duties on the right side of the infield. His prime responsibilities are to play in the "hole" between first and second—the geographical area between first and second—to cover second base when a runner is attempting to steal from first,* and to participate in the double play, about which, more later.

3. THE SHORTSTOP

Shortstop is, most experts agree, the key infield position.** Playing in the hole between second and

---

mine, and I am spared the burden of having to worry about his stealing against *me*. It is a baseball truism that most steals are made against the pitcher. If a pitcher lets a baserunner take a long lead—usually because the pitcher is concentrating on what he's going to throw to the batter—it becomes well-nigh impossible for the catcher to throw the runner out.

* In a situation in which a steal attempt is likely, the decision as to whether the second baseman or shortstop will take the throw to second is reached by agreement between the two players. On some plays, the second baseman will cover; on others, the shortstop. If a right-handed hitter—who traditionally hits to the *left* side of the infield—is up, then the second baseman will cover. If a left-handed hitter is at bat, the shortstop will usually take the throw. But heed the word "usually." Some hitters are so skilled at manipulating the bat that they can hit to either the right or left side. If a talented hitter knows who will cover second on an attempted steal, he will certainly try to hit the pitch to the spot vacated by the infielder—whether short or second. So the shortstop and second baseman establish an irregular pattern for their coverage, signaling each other from behind the shield of their gloves.

** The experts who play first, second, and third base will be inclined to disagree.

third, the shortstop must have speed and a strong arm. He has to be fast to cover his position adequately, to range left and right in pursuit of ground balls or low line drives. And he needs a powerful arm because he must make the longest throw required of any infielder. That throw comes about as a result of a classic fielding play—the litmus test that separates the premier shortstop from the merely adequate. Here it is.

A right-handed batter hits a hard ground ball in the hole between short and second. The third baseman, who has been assiduously guarding the left-field line—this is analogous to the first baseman guarding the right-field line, remember?—makes a valiant but futile effort to get the ball, sprawling full length on the ground. Meanwhile, the shortstop is scooting to his right to back up the third baseman. Without exception, every major-league shortstop is right-handed, so his glove hand is his left, requiring him to make a backhand stop of the ball—a celebrated phrase which means that a player reaches across his body with his glove to make the stop. He reaches the ball "deep in the hole" (on the edge of the outfield grass) and, having fielded the grounder, must now throw the batter out at first, no mean feat from where he finds himself. In addition, the shortstop is off balance, leaning *away* from first base. He must straighten up, transfer his weight to his right foot, and release a strong throw to first.

The step-by-step explanation of this classic play is also a classic example of the frustration of writing about baseball. This play—the shortstop going deep into the hole to field a ground ball and throw the batter out at first—is an exercise in fluid motion. But in analysis it assumes a stop-start, herky-jerky character that is completely foreign to the graceful symmetry of reality.

The shortstop tends to be a peppery sort of player, a vocal leader on the field. The position is so important that in the balance of assets of each player—in terms of fielding and hitting—a good shortstop may be carried even if, as the saying goes, he can't hit his weight.* This isn't to say that shortstops, by definition, can't hit. But it underscores the defensive contribution to his team that a good shortstop can make, and the importance that managers assign to the position.

4. THE THIRD BASEMAN

We last saw the fourth member of the infield quartet stretched at full length on the ground in an attempt to field a ground ball. Reason and fairness demand that we dust off the third baseman and give him equal time. Third base is called "the hot corner." The name is derived from the fact that the third-base corner can be a very busy place indeed.

---

* "Hit his weight" is a hoary baseball phrase referring to the failure of a player to keep his average on a par with his weight. A batting average is computed by dividing the number of *official* times at bat for each player into the number of hits he has made. If a player has been at bat 30 times and collected 10 hits, his batting average is 10 divided by 30: .333. A player who got a hit on every official at-bat is batting 1.000. As you can see, "can't hit his weight" is something of an insult, unless a player is gargantuan. Now, I'm not gargantuan—I scale 195 pounds—but in 1968 I hit .170, and I'm considered a good hitting pitcher. However, as my favorite fan will eventually explain, pitchers aren't expected to be good hitters. Perhaps that's why we're so vain about the infrequent hits we do get.

Why?

Well, there are more right-handed hitters than left-handed hitters. Also, any hitter will get more power from his swing if the bat has moved through the greatest possible arc.* And the maximum amount of bat travel for a right-handed hitter will be such as to send the ball screaming to the left side of the infield. Added to this compound of baseball and the laws of physics is the frequent necessity for the third baseman to play "up"—closer than normal—to the plate. As you can see, the hot corner is accurately named. The third baseman guards the line against the chance of a ball being smashed through between himself and the bag. If he can't flag it down, the ball will almost certainly go for two bases—a double.

The hot-corner resident also must be alert for a slow roller or a bunt. Poised on the balls of his feet, occasionally tapping his right hand into his glove, he leans forward in the characteristic infielder's crouch, alert for any one of several developments.

* Getting maximum power from the batter's swing at the moment of contact with the ball, obedience to the laws of physics, and the rich store of at-the-plate folklore all boil down to one word: *pull*. When a hitter pulls, he is actually getting ahead of the pitch. Thus, a right-handed pull hitter has his power concentrated to *left* field, because maximum bat travel will direct the ball there. In extreme cases, a hitter may be referred to as a "dead pull" hitter, meaning that he is absolutely incapable of hitting to right. If a right-handed hitter swings "late," he will hit to right, but the length of his swing will be curtailed, with a resultant loss of power. As always, the directions are reversed for a left-handed hitter—who pulls to right field. I suspect we will confront this question again during a later chapter on hitting.

Suppose the batter takes a full swing but manages only to trickle the ball up the third-base line. From his normal fielding position behind or abreast of the bag, the third baseman charges in. In a single motion he must make a barehand pickup of the ball and, while still off balance, release a strong and accurate throw to first. Fielding a bunt requires the same agility and dexterity.*

5. THE DOUBLE PLAY

A double play is made when, on a continuing play, two outs are recorded. By far the largest number of such plays involve the second baseman, the shortstop, and the first baseman.

Let us look at a classic example. There is a runner on first and, of course, there are fewer than two outs. The batter hits a ground ball to short. The shortstop fields it and races a couple of steps to his left. As he nears second base he flips the ball to the second baseman, who has charged over to take the toss. (Note that the second baseman must have one foot on the bag at the time he receives the throw from short.) As the runner from first slides into second in a cloud of dust, the second baseman pivots sharply and throws to first. "Out" signals the umpire at second. "Out" is the definitive call at first.

---

* In bunting, the hitter does *not* swing at a pitch. He holds the bat loosely, and gently meets the thrown ball. The result is, or should be, a ball which rolls slowly and tantalizingly beyond the reach of the pitcher and infielders. There are different kinds of bunts and different reasons for bunting—all of which, I assume, we will eventually explore. By the way, a hitter "lays down a bunt" or "dumps a bunt"—and sometimes, even in a game distinguished by its colorful argot, simply "bunts."

Two outs have been recorded on one continuing play: the double play or, as it is familiarly called, the DP.*

Let's look at another variation of the double play. With a runner on first and fewer than two out, the batter hits a ground ball to the first baseman. The first baseman steps on the bag. He then throws to the shortstop, who has moved over to take his throw at second. But the shortstop must tag the runner, because the runner is no longer forced, the force having been removed when the first baseman stepped on first, thus retiring the batter.

This play can also work the other way. With fewer than two out and a runner on first, the batter hits a ground ball to the first baseman, who throws to second. The shortstop takes the throw, steps on second, and throws to the first baseman, who has returned to his base. In this case, the runner is forced at second, and a tag is not required.

Not all double plays are executed by the shortstop, second baseman, and first baseman. In fact, not all DPs take place in the infield. (For example, an outfielder can make the catch of a drive that a runner thought would surely be a hit. If the throw from the outfield gets to the base that the runner left before the runner manages to return,

* The shortstop and second baseman are often referred to as "the double-play combination." There are several basic principles of baseball involved in the DP. The first is that a runner can be *forced*. That is, if first base is occupied, the batter hitting the ground ball is forcing the runner who was on first to move to second. And the out at second is recorded merely when the second baseman (in possession of the ball) touches the second-base bag. In any situation where a runner is forced *at any base*, it is not necessary to tag the runner.

the runner is out. In this case, baseball parlance says that the runner was "doubled off.") But most DPs do occur in the infield and depend on the talented gloves of the second baseman and his partner in denial, the shortstop.

The Outfield

Broadly, we have now covered the prime responsibilities of the infielders—and no doubt have incurred the outrage of 75 per cent of them. All major-league infielders have the ability to make a difficult play, a tough chance, look easy. And most can make impossible plays, the great plays that bring a roar of approval from the stands and a frustrated shake of the head from the batter deprived of a hit.

But suppose a ground ball gets through the infield, or the batter hits a fly ball? The ball and the action then enter the province of the outfield.

Outfielders are sometimes called "pickets"—a name derived, I suppose, from picketing a horse to allow him to graze. And although the outfield itself is occasionally referred to as "the pasture," the outfielders have little opportunity to chew the grass—or the fat.

1. THE CENTER FIELDER

The defensive outfield specialist is the center fielder. His is the largest section of turf to be covered laterally, and of course center field is the deepest section of the ball park. By unwritten law, the center fielder takes every ball he can get. That is, if the right fielder and the center fielder converge, the other man usually gives way to the center fielder.

By reason of the sheer size of the territory he

patrols, you would rightly expect the center fielder to be fast. And he is. The speed of the outfielders doesn't show up in the box scores,* but is often silently reflected there. After all, before you can catch a ball you have to be able to catch up to it. If a team's three outfielders are swift, they will certainly deprive their opponents of numerous hits. And the same speed will enable an outfielder to keep a single from becoming an extra-base hit—a double—or a double from becoming a triple or even an inside-the-park home run. This outfield art form is known as "cutting the ball off."

For example, the batter lines the ball sharply to left, heading toward the alley.** The center fielder gets a good jump on the ball—with the crack of the bat he has computed its direction, velocity, and landing point—and races over, getting the ball on the first or second hop. Hence, he has cut the ball off—prevented it from rolling through.

Except for the catcher and the first baseman, all ballplayers use roughly the same kind of glove— large yet flexible, with a deep pocket and massive webbing between the thumb and first finger.† In

* Box scores are statistical summaries of every game, showing at-bats, runs, hits and errors for every player; the winning and losing pitchers; and other tabulated information. During the season, the sports page of your paper is sprinkled with them.
** The alley referred to here has neither garbage cans nor a back door. It is the left-field power alley, the channel between the left fielder and the center fielder. As you may have already guessed, there is also a right-field alley, between the right fielder and the center fielder.
† Actually, the infielders' gloves are a trifle smaller than those used by outfielders. This is a matter of choice, not penalty. The smaller glove—with less webbing, and perhaps a shallower pocket—helps pre-

essence, the glove is so good that an outfielder should be able to catch any ball he can get to. In fact, it is the glove—and more precisely, the webbing in the glove—which makes a successful acrobatic catch possible. I don't mean to suggest that outfielders aren't talented athletes. They are.* But the diving, tumbling catches we occasionally see—which might be more at home in a gymnastic competition—could not be accomplished without today's formidable glove.

I vividly remember one outfield catch. The Cardinals were playing the Chicago Cubs, and Ron Santo, the Cubs' third baseman, was up. My husband threw him a hanging curve which Mr. Santo drilled to the deepest part of the ball park. Curt Flood, then the Cardinals' brilliant center fielder, turned his back to the plate and raced back, back, way back, watching the ball over his shoulder as he ran. In front of the center-field wall, Curt Flood took a last running stride, literally climbing up the wall, his momentum giving him a precarious balance in the air. In that fraction of a second as he hung suspended above the field, he raised his gloved hand and speared the ball inches away from the gray concrete.

Of course, it may have been Flood's glove that enabled him to catch the ball, but it was his speed, reflexes, and eyesight that enabled him to judge where the ball would be and get to it. And let us not forget his determination to make the impossible

---

vent a ground ball, once snared, from getting "buried" in the glove. Thus the infielder can extract the ball from the glove smoothly and swiftly, without delaying his throw.

* I love my outfielders. And my infielders. So does every pitcher.

catch possible. Such a catch does more than deprive the opposition of a double or triple and, if there are runners on base, several runs. It can take away the enemy's momentum and, simultaneously, give the fielder's team an enormous emotional lift.

2. THE RIGHT FIELDER

If all outfielders can make good use of speed afoot, equally so can they benefit from being well armed. The pun may be unforgivable, but a strong arm is, in the parlance of today's uneasy world, an effective deterrent. This is especially true of the right fielder.

In "The Field" I talked briefly about the importance of the right fielder's arm in preventing a runner from taking an extra base—going from first to third on a single—or discouraging a speedy batter from stretching a single into a double. Here again, the threat of what might happen is sufficient to prevent a runner or batter from taking a chance. And though it may not show up in the box score, the right fielder's "howitzer" can prevent a team from scoring.

From a defensive point of view, baseball is a grudging game. If we can't get a batter out, then we hope to see him advance no farther than first base—or, more grudgingly, second; or, with a painful grimace, third. The sequence of progressive denial is important because it underscores the logic of the game. It is easiest to score from third base; harder from second; harder still from first. So defensive factors which retard the base-by-base progress of runners—such as the speed and throwing ability of the outfielders—can affect the final score every bit as much as the more obvious exploits of the hitters.

3. THE LEFT FIELDER

I have not intended to neglect the left fielder. He can be as fast as any other outfielder.* He may have just as strong an arm. His may be the surest hands of those that seek after line drives and fly balls. But as a highly generalized statement, the left fielder does not usually have as strong an arm as his companions on the picket line. However, his arm must be accurate, for he is most often the key figure in one of baseball's most exciting dramas, the play at the plate.

Remember that a majority of hitters are right-handed, with a tendency to hit to left field. Thus there will be many occasions when there is a runner on second base and the hitter lines a single to left. If the left fielder makes a clean pickup of the ball, he will try to nail the runner at the plate.

4. THE PLAY AT THE PLATE

As the outfielder scoops the ball up and uncorks his throw, the runner from second turns third and streaks for home. Wherever you are in the stadium, you can see the impending convergence of the runner and the incoming ball. Depending on how deep the left fielder was, his throw may come in on the fly, or it may bounce once or twice before reaching the catcher.

To improve his visibility, the catcher has ripped off his mask. He stands in front of the plate, slightly up the line toward third—blocking the plate. He is challenging the runner, who can elect to slide under or around the catcher or barrel over him.

* He certainly can. Even faster. Lou Brock, as Cardinal left fielder, led the major leagues in stolen bases in 1966, 1967, and 1968.

If the throw arrives in time, the catcher will have to tag the runner—who isn't, of course, forced—and he must hold on to the ball, despite the impact as the runner crashes into him. If the throw is wide, or the catcher drops the ball, the runner scores.

One of the attractions of this play is that you can see it as it develops. And to my eyes, at least, there is a fierce fascination in the way two unrelated actions converge at the plate. The play at home inevitably brings the fans to their feet in a noisy chorus of encouragement to the runner or the outfielder—depending upon which ballplayer is wearing the home team's uniform.

A variation of the play at the plate involves the "relay man." In this case a runner is usually trying to score from first on a long double or perhaps a triple. The hitter has driven the ball up one of the alleys, or perhaps banged a long drive off the scoreboard in deep right center (or left center) field. In any case, an outfielder has had to pursue the ball into some distant part of the ball park. At that distance from home, no human can throw the ball to the plate. So an infielder goes out into short right field (or center or left), and the outfielder throws to him. The infielder then relays the throw to the catcher.

The teamwork between the infielders and outfielders is evidenced in yet another play, this one involving the "cut-off man." Let us return to our tireless runner from second, charging homeward on a single to left. If the left fielder's throw goes all the way home, the hitter, after rounding first, will go on to second. To avoid this—particularly in a case in which the throw home will clearly *not*

arrive in time to prevent the runner from scoring—
the outfielders are taught to make their throws at
a height which, as the ball reaches the infield, is
low enough to be caught by an appointed infielder
—the cut-off man. He can choose to let the throw
continue home, or he can intercept it and hope to
catch the hitter attempting to sneak into second.
At the very least, cutting off the throw home will
confine the hitter to a single and prevent him from
going to second on the throw.

A hallowed baseball adage says that to play
winning baseball a team must be "strong through
the middle." This refers to strength in the center
of the diamond—behind the plate, on the mound,
at short and second, in center field. This doesn't
mean that the players at first and third and in left
and right are all thumbs. Rather, it means that
the players at those positions may be fielders of
ordinary major-league caliber—which is very high
indeed—whose (comparative) weakness in the
field is more than compensated for by their strength
at the plate. Whatever amassed talent a team may
boast, it will be frustrated in its quest for a
championship unless it is strong through the middle.

Defensive Averages
The defensive profile of a player is reflected in his
fielding average. This portrait of in-the-field excellence is based on four elements: putouts, assists,
chances, and errors.

A *putout* is recorded whenever a fielder catches
a fly ball or line drive, whether fair or foul; catches
a thrown ball which retires a batter or runner;
tags a runner when the runner is off the base to

which he is legally entitled. There are a number of "special situations" in which various players are credited with a putout under strange circumstances, but these anomalies of scoring need not concern us now. Broadly, a putout is simply the specific credit for an out.

An *assist* is recorded for each player who helps to achieve a putout. Any player who throws or deflects a ball on a play in which a putout results gets an assist. For example, suppose the batter hits a hard ground ball back at the pitcher, who manages to get his glove on the ball, but only enough to deflect the ball toward short. But the alert shortstop fields the ball and throws to first in time to get the batter. The statistics of baseball credit the pitcher with an assist, the shortstop with an assist, and the first baseman with a putout.

A *chance* is simply a fielding opportunity—a chance to receive credit for an assist or a putout.

An *error* is a misplay—a fumble of a ground ball, a muff of a catch, or a wild throw. An error is always charged to someone whenever the "life" of the batter has been prolonged, quite regardless of whether the batter gets on base. For example, suppose the batter hits a pop-up in foul ground behind the plate. The catcher rips off his mask and camps underneath waiting for it. Inexplicably, he drops the ball. The catcher is charged with an error because the batter is still, in baseball parlance, "alive."

Now suppose, in the same example, that the catcher trips over his own feet and never touches the ball. Even so, he may still be charged with an error. In this case, he has committed an error of omission rather than commission.

To compute a player's fielding average, we must

first add his putouts, assists, and errors. The sum of these is called his "total chances"—the total of defensive plays in which he has participated. We then divide total chances into the sum of putouts and assists (without including the errors) and carry the answer out to three decimal places. The result is a player's fielding average. A player who handles all his chances with flawless excellence is fielding 1.000—pronounced "a thousand."

The responsibility of deciding who is credited with an assist or a putout—or charged with an error—belongs to the "official scorer." He is a baseball writer who, on a rotating basis, takes his turn in the ball park at sitting in judgment on play in the field. He is always from the home club's city—that is, he is a newspaperman assigned to the club which is playing at home.

Red Barber, the gentlemanly broadcaster who at various times manned the microphones for the Cincinnati Reds, the Brooklyn Dodgers, and the New York Yankees, was fond of pointing out to his radio and (later) television audience that "baseball is only a game to the fans." The Old Redhead was referring to the fact that baseball is a career to professional ballplayers. And in this connection the official scorer has a peculiar—and, to the players, vital—significance.

The ruling of an official scorer has a direct effect on a player's professional excellence as reflected by his fielding average, batting average, or ERA.* Baseball writers are just as human as

* ERA stands for the pitcher's "earned-run average" per nine-inning game. An earned run is one for which the pitcher, *as a result of his pitching*, is responsible. Runs which score as a result of errors are not included in the ERA, since they came about as a result of a

any other breed of fan. Moreover, the writer's
life is baseball, and it is hardly surprising that he
is a staunch supporter of the club whose fortunes
he faithfully reports for his local readers, whether
that club is in New York or Pittsburgh or Atlanta
or Los Angeles. The writer, as a fan, wants the
players on the local team to hit well and field
well and pitch well. Consciously or otherwise, the
official scorer sometimes falls prey to his unofficial
feeling of team loyalty. So it may happen that
when the home team is batting the official scorer
gives the hitter a base hit when a fielder should
have been given an error. Of course, this occurs
only on questionable plays, those in which the
scorer has some legitimate discretion. But in such
situations personal loyalty not infrequently super-
sedes impartial judgment. Thus, the batting average of the hitter is undeservedly inflated by that
"hit," and the fielder, who should have received an
error, goes unpunished. And if the hitter in our test
case should score, the pitcher will be charged with
an earned run, for didn't the batter get on base
by getting a hit? By the same token, had the batter
gotten on base as a result of an error, the run
would be unearned, and there would be no resultant damage to the pitcher's ERA. I am not suggesting in any way that official scorers are evil
or grossly unfair. But I have watched enough ball
games to know that they are secretly just as much

---

fielding lapse by a player—even if that player was the
pitcher—rather than through the opposition's hitting.
Once a team has had the opportunity to make three
outs in an inning, but has prolonged the inning by
making one or more errors, all subsequent runs are
unearned.

fans as any of us—and not always so secretly, at that.

If I were the official scorer I would certainly be tempted to make quite certain that no one ever scored an earned run off *my* husband. Which brings us to our next consideration: the battery.

The Battery

A pitcher is the fielder designated to deliver the ball to the batter. The catcher is the fielder who takes his position back of the home base.—*Official Baseball Rules*

The Pitcher

He leans forward on the mound, staring intently at the catcher. Holding the ball behind his back, he nods his head in agreement with the catcher's sign. The hitter waits, frozen in rigid concentration. Only his bat moves; cocked and ready, it twitches restlessly, as though impatient to begin its swing.

1. THE BRUSHBACK PITCH

The pitcher begins his windup. He pumps once, then again. His leg kicks high, and around comes his arm, delivering the ball in a blurred white streak toward the plate. For an instant the batter remains motionless. Then, his pose and poise simultaneously shattered, he catapults himself out of the batter's box and sprawls in the dirt.

Such incidents occur with strange regularity in baseball. They are not always accidental—not always attributable to the pitcher's slipping as he delivers the ball, or to an otherwise errant pitch. Sometimes they are the visible results of a pitcher's tactical advantage as the wielder of an enormously important psychological weapon: fear.

A baseball weighs 5 ounces. A major-league fast ball rockets to the plate at speeds of up to 100 miles per hour. The batter doesn't have to be a math whiz to complete the equation: getting hit by a pitch hurts. And besides the pain, there is the threat of serious injury—of an entire season of play lost or of a career abruptly and tragically terminated.

All of us share a self-protective reflex which urgently guards us against painful collisions, with a baseball or anything else. If you are standing on the edge of the platform when a train pulls in, you step back. You may *know* that the train isn't going to overlap the platform's edge, but your self-protective reflex isn't convinced. The same reflex is present in the mind of a hitter. Only the major-leaguer's mental discipline enables him to suppress the reflex and stay at the plate time after time without "bailing out." But even though the reflex is controlled, it still lurks in the dark recesses of the batter's mind. The pitcher knows it and will exploit that fear whenever he deems it necessary.*

The fight erupted in the fifth inning, though the pressure behind it had been building since the be-

---

* There can be several explanations for a pitch that sends a batter lurching out of the box. He may have been crowding the plate—standing very close to the plate—so that a normal inside pitch forces him to retreat. Or he may have been expecting a pitch away—on the outside of the plate—and been leaning out over the plate when, to his surprise, the pitch was inside. Or the ball may have slipped from the pitcher's grasp, or simply have been badly thrown.

ginning of the game. It was July 3, 1967. The Cardinals were playing the Cincinnati Reds in St. Louis. My husband was pitching, and my tension —the standard accompaniment of any baseball player's wife watching her husband at work—had been largely dissipated when the Cardinals scored seven runs in the very first inning. Reassured by this commanding lead, I had settled back in my seat, occasionally allowing my thoughts to turn to what we would have for dinner. But I had reckoned without the Reds' frustration at being so far behind so early in the game.

In the third inning the Cards' second baseman, Julian Javier, was knocked down by a pitch. Then

---

And, let us make no bones about it, there are also two other possibilities: the "brushback" pitch and the "knockdown."

The first of these is absolutely essential. The brushback is designed to keep the hitter on his toes—literally, in the sense that a hitter who crowds the plate has excellent bat reach for outside pitches. If a pitcher lets a hitter stay in that position, the pitcher is giving the batter an enormous advantage, and he won't be pitching in the major leagues very long. The personal struggle between pitcher and batter is just that: a personal war. The brushback tells the hitter that you are aware. The pitch is accurately named, for its intention is to brush the hitter back from the plate.

The knockdown is supposedly intended to hit the batter. I say "supposedly" because often the pitch is thrown merely with the intention of sending the batter sprawling. A pitcher can, after all, hit a batter with a baseball any time he wants to—not officially, of course, since the rules expressly forbid it. But any pitcher is technically capable of plunking a batter in the ribs. I think the one valid reason for throwing at a hitter is in response to the opposing pitcher's throwing at your teammates. In such cases a manager may specifically direct his pitcher to retaliate. Usually left fielder Lou Brock was hit by a pitch in the fourth. Lulled into a sense of security by the big lead Bob's teammates had given him, I had progressed from appetizer to entrée and was musing over the options available for dessert. Speculating on the comparative virtues of apple pie versus blueberry, I watched Robert pitch to the Reds' Tony Perez. The first delivery sailed over the top of his head, sending Perez collapsing in a scramble of arms and legs flat on his back. On the next pitch Perez hit a towering infield pop, which he ran out.* He turned at first and, as the

---

that explicit instruction isn't necessary. You can get pretty angry and frustrated sitting in the dugout when your friends and teammates are being victimized at the plate. Eventually it becomes apparent that a pitcher is throwing *at*, not *to*, the hitter. Just so many pitches can slip, just so many batters can be crowding the plate, before it is transparently obvious that what is happening could not be accidental. Then the umpire behind the plate warns the pitcher. Should the warning have to be repeated, the punishment is stern: ejection from the game.

How does the sequence of knockdowns get started in the first place? It may be the result of an old feud. Or, in a fit of pique, an immature pitcher may decide to punish a hitter for having hit a home run the last time he was up. Or perhaps on a preceding play a runner crashed into the second baseman with what the pitcher thinks was unnecessary force, so he knocks the next batter down.

As I said, I consider retaliation the only valid reason for throwing the knockdown. But the brushback is a legitimate weapon, and we poor pitchers have only a very few of those.

* A popup has nothing to do with abusing a paternal figure. It's an infield fly ball, a very easy out. There is also a verbal form of the word, as in "He popped to third," or "He pops the ball up." All ballplayers are instructed to run hard whenever they hit the ball, even

catch was made, started slowly back to his dugout. On the way he presumably said something. Presumably, because with fifty thousand screaming, jeering, applauding fans, it is impossible to hear anything. I presume also that Mr. Gibson replied to Mr. Perez—no doubt in the same vein.*

At any rate, Perez changed his course and started for the mound. Before he got there, Orlando Cepeda, who was then the Cardinal first baseman, intercepted him and attempted to mollify him. I think his role of peacemaker might have been successful, but at this fateful moment a player from the Cincinnati bullpen charged onto the field, screaming at Cepeda. He met him and received a couple of left hooks and a right cross. Immediately both dugouts emptied and fights broke out all over the field. Dinner had long ago been forgotten, and I stood up on my seat in a vain attempt to locate my husband. Of course everybody else was standing on his seat, which didn't prevent those behind me from screaming, "Down in front," with high-decibel urgency that would have done justice to Paul Revere.

---

on what should be an easy out, for there is always the possibility of error. This is "running out" a play. Statistically, of course, the chances of a fielder making an error are slim—even slimmer when the chance is an easy one. But it does happen. And woe betide the batter who *is* out because he didn't run hard on a ball that he *thought* was a sure out and was—but only because of the batter's lack of hustle. When he returns to the dugout the manager will blister his ears—and perhaps his wallet as well, with a fine.

* I don't really know what Mr. Perez said. Honestly. I do know what I said: "Come and get me." Alas, the invitation was, as you will see, accepted by a number of his teammates as well.

I later learned that Bob had somehow found his way into the Cincinnati dugout, where he defended himself against three attackers.* This was the biggest, most all-inclusive baseball fight I've ever seen. It was particularly galling, of course, to be trapped in the stands—a noncombatant position of complete safety but also one which made me writhe in frustration. For although I have attempted to treat the matter lightly, I was, of course, deeply concerned.**

Perhaps in a later chapter we can examine some of the peculiarities of life for a ballplayer's wife. But now I see that the game is about to resume, and a batter is digging in at the plate.

The fear (no matter how successfully controlled) that the batter carries to the plate is one of a pitcher's tactical weapons. There are others, which the pitcher must bring to the mound. First among these is control.

2. CONTROL

A pitcher must be able to throw strikes. This doesn't mean he has to throw the ball straight down the middle, over the heart of the plate. On the contrary, he must be able to pitch to spots— inside and across the letters (of the uniform of the batter), or across the knees and the outside corner, and vice versa. Good control is a prerequisite of good pitching.

Look at Diagram No. 2, a diagram of the strike

* In truth, I don't know who the three guys were with whom I traded punches. I gave a few and got a lot. They might even have been my own teammates simply trying to restrain me.
** So much so, in fact, that my wife was incapable of preparing dinner that night. We ate out.

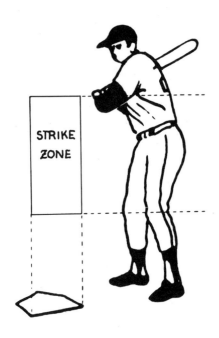

Diagram No. 2

zone, which is the space over home plate between
the batter's armpits and the top of his knees when
he assumes his normal stance. It shows basic
pitching "spots" for a right-handed hitter. Note
that the designations "inside" and "outside" would
be reversed for a left-handed hitter.

3. THE FAST BALL

Broadly, all pitches are divided into two categories: fast balls and breaking balls. A fast ball
is just that: a pitch thrown as hard—that is, as
fast—as the pitcher can. It is the hummer, the

blazer, the smoker of the broadcaster's description.

A good fast ball doesn't come in absolutely flat. Or at least it doesn't appear to. The faster a ball is thrown, the less time is available in which gravity can pull the ball down. Thus a fast ball doesn't respond to this downward influence as much as the batter thinks it should. In the hitter's mind, and to the hitter's eye, the fast ball has a "hop." It rises, or the hitter thinks it rises, as it crosses the plate. Illusion or delusion, the real or apparent movement of a fast ball is what hitters mean when they say, "He has a live fast ball."

You can't really tell from the stands how hard a pitcher throws, or the suddenness with which the pitched ball appears at the plate, and with what incredible velocity. I can, because of an experience at the Omaha YMCA playground. During the off-season Robert would occasionally go to the playground and talk baseball with the kids. Naturally the kids would ask him to throw a few pitches, but no one was willing to catch them. I volunteered, and one day I put on slacks and sneakers and went down to the playground, a catcher's mitt tucked under my arm. We got to the field, and I assumed what I still think was the epitome of a catcher's crouch and pounded my glove with professional ease. A foot or so behind me was a brick wall which would serve as a backstop if I missed a pitch. I yelled something encouraging to my battery mate, who wound up and threw.

Blind instinct made me lift the glove as the ball, a blurred streak of white, rocketed in on me. The ball exploded in my glove, sending me flying backward to land on my bruised dignity against the wall. Robert *says* he threw a change-up, but I know better. Proof that I do know better is that I will never catch for him again.

4. THE CURVE

If the fast ball is the basic pitch, the curve is not far behind in importance. Unlike the fast ball, which by definition is delivered as fast as a pitcher can throw, the curve can be thrown at varying speeds and with different degrees of "break"—the amount of deviation from a straight line. The principal characteristic of the curve ball is its downward break—down and away from a right-handed hitter *if thrown by a right-handed pitcher*; down and away from a port-side swinger *if thrown by a lefty*.

There are fast curves and slow curves. In general, the slow curve breaks more, because, as you will remember, the longer it takes the ball to travel from the pitcher's hand to the plate, the longer gravity has a chance to pull the ball down.

5. THE SLIDER

A relatively new breaking pitch is the slider. Think of it as a cross between a fast ball and a curve. A slider looks like a fast ball as it approaches the plate, but it then veers away, either inside or outside. Unlike the curve, which breaks abruptly down, the slider breaks either left or right, with a downward slant, but not as sharp a slant as a curve.

6. THE SCREWBALL

Another breaking pitch is the screwball, or scroogie. It is endorsed mostly by left-handed pitchers because its action is the reverse of a curve. Thrown by a lefty, the screwball breaks away from right-handed hitters. Because there are so many more right-handed hitters than left-handed ones, the screwball is an effective pitch for a southpaw. Right-handed pitchers have less statistical need to find a pitch that breaks away from left-handed hitters, because the latter are a minority.

One reason for the reluctance of many pitchers to throw the screwball is that it puts an extra strain on the pitcher's arm, especially around the elbow.

7. THE KNUCKLEBALL

Another breaking pitch is the knuckleball, or knuckler. The ball is gripped by either the fingertips or knuckles and does not spin. It arrives at the plate in a state of near exhaustion. Because of its lack of spin and velocity, it is powerfully affected by even very minor changes in air currents and air pressure. There are some pitchers who throw a relatively fast knuckler, but the pitch is essentially a slow one.

8. THE SINKER

Yet another breaking pitch that you will hear sports announcers and fans refer to is the sinker, a variety of fast ball or slider with a downward break. The exactitude of the description is really quite accurate. Some pitchers have a fast ball which just naturally sinks as it crosses the plate. Others, for some reason, throw a slider that has a natural downward break—thus, a sinker.*

---

* The characteristics of a pitch are determined by how the ball is held in the hand—fingers across the seams of the ball or with the seams, in the palm of the hand or with the fingertips or knuckles; and how it is delivered—with wrist straight or bent, so as to achieve

9. THE CHANGE-OF-PACE

Another basic pitch is the change-of-pace, or change-up, or simply change. This is, as the name signifies, a slow pitch. It is really the obverse of the fast ball, and is used to exaggerate the apparent speed of the fast ball. Conversely, the fast ball exaggerates the apparent slowness of the change-up. It is most important that this pitch be thrown with the same motion that a pitcher uses to throw a fast ball or curve. Otherwise the hitter will not be surprised but only gratified because he knows that a slow and easy-to-hit delivery is on its way. The change-up, then, is a contrast, especially effective after a series of sliders and fast balls, when the hitter's reflexes and timing are conditioned to fast pitches.

By way of review: A pitcher's repertoire must, absolutely *must*, include three pitches: a fast ball, a change-up, and a breaking pitch of some sort (curve, slider, screwball).*

---

the chosen kind of spin on the ball. It is more or less unnecessary for the fan to be aware of all the details, but the following example of what a small change in technique can accomplish may be interesting. One day as I was practicing I discovered that I could achieve two distinct results by simply varying my grip on the ball when I threw a fast ball. Holding the ball across the seams, I could make the ball sail away from a right-handed hitter. Holding the ball with the seams, I could make the ball sink and tail into—toward—a right-handed hitter. Just a simple change, but the results were startlingly different.

* My learned wife's generalization is correct, as a generalization, for starting pitchers—those who begin the game and, if things go well, finish it. But if things don't go well a specialist is called in from the bullpen: the relief pitcher. If he does his job, he

Up till now, we have been discussing *legal* pitches, ones the rules of baseball officially permit a pitcher to throw. There are also a great many illegal pitches, officially outlawed but still very much in use, if not in evidence.

10. THE SPITBALL

The most famous illegal pitch is the spitball, or spitter. As the name suggests, it is a pitch in which saliva is furtively applied to the ball. The result is a fast ball that breaks with astounding and unexpected sharpness. The rules expressly forbid the pitcher to "go to his mouth," but perspiration from hand, wrist, or forehead can be used slyly to anoint the baseball, as can hair oil and a variety of other substances. The "emery ball" (a ball rubbed with sandpaper) achieves the same result—an unpredictable break.

It is my unofficial estimate that no more than one-quarter of the pitchers in the major leagues

---

brings relief to the manager and to the starting pitcher, whose victory he preserves. Time was when the relief pitcher was simply a pitcher who wasn't as good as a starting pitcher. But not any more. Today a relief pitcher is a specialist at putting out fires and often gets the nickname of fireman. Not infrequently the reliever has one great pitch, perhaps a sinker that will usually result in the ball being hit on the ground so that his teammates can start a double play and get out of the inning. Or perhaps he throws a knuckler —and perhaps only a knuckler—that butterflies its way to the plate, leaving the batters in a state of frustration and exhaustion as they fruitlessly fan the air with their bats. Or perhaps he has a delivery—a pattern of windup and throw—which is particularly difficult for a right-handed batter to hit. If so, he will be brought into the game only to pitch to a right-handed hitter.

occasionally throw a spitter. But before you thunder with outrage at the wickedness of such criminal moundsmen, consider this. The spitter, or any other illegal pitch, is only as good as the pitcher who throws it. In the hands of a good pitcher, a spitter can be an effective weapon. For an artless pitcher, it's simply another way to get in trouble.

11. THE HAZARDS OF PITCHING

In cataloguing the variety of pitches seen in the major leagues with some regularity, I have painted only one side of the picture. There is another, more gloomy one—particularly if your husband is a pitcher. I refer to the inventory of mistakes, any one of which can result in the batter's getting good wood on the ball and going into his home-run trot around the bases. Let's examine some of the possibilities of catastrophe, horror by horror.

The fast ball is, as previously indicated, the basic pitch because, in addition to setting up other pitches, it also gets a goodly number of strikeouts and, if it is a sinker, ground balls that may wind up as outs or double plays. The fast ball is also the easiest pitch to control. If the fast ball is fast enough—a quality which varies according to the capacity of each pitcher—it is, all things considered, about the safest of all deliveries. But if it isn't fast enough it will travel up, up and away, because to the force of the batter's swing is added the velocity of the fast ball itself.

The curve ball is a most effective pitch *when it curves*. Not all curves do, though. When a curve doesn't break fast or far enough, it is said to "hang." Because a curve is a slower pitch than a fast ball, the batter has more time to take aim at it. Therefore, if the curve fails to curve, it is a particularly easy pitch to hit. To minimize the chance of impending tragedy, pitchers are taught to throw only low curves that pass through the lower portion of the strike zone. A high curve is a plea for early retirement—of the pitcher, not the batter.

The change-up is designed to fool the hitter. Its effect is one of exaggerated slowness by comparison with other pitches. If the hitter isn't fooled, the pitcher (and the pitcher's wife) can only pray.

It is my estimate that more home runs are hit off sliders than off any other pitch. Why? The hard slider is a fast ball with something taken off it. The slight but significant reduction in speed should be compensated for by the break of the pitch. But if a slider doesn't slide, it's just a fast ball that isn't quite fast enough. The word "hard" is added by every broadcaster I've ever heard, even though the slider *must* be thrown hard; there is no slow slider.

The screwball is a difficult pitch to learn to throw and one that can be painful, even physically harmful, to deliver.

The knuckleball is the most difficult pitch to hit, and the most difficult pitch to control. Neither the pitcher nor the catcher has any idea of which way it will go. Therefore it is a great pitch for a runner to steal on. And with men on base it often results in a wild pitch or the catcher's equivalent misplay, a passed ball. On either of these the runner or runners can advance on the bases, and perhaps even score.

Enough! This recital of calamities is too much

for me.* These are some of the many ways in which a pitcher can get into hot water—specifically, the hot water in the clubhouse showers—long before the game is over. Additionally, you have now learned the meaning of the ominous baseball phrase "heading for an early shower."

12. BALLS AND STRIKES

Like so much of baseball, pitching has a mathematical foundation, though it has a superstructure of emotion. That mathematical character is summed up in the familiar question posed by one fan to another, "What's the count?"

The question refers to the number of balls and strikes at that particular moment. It is a question that every pitcher can always answer, because the count is one of the elements that determine what his pitching strategy will be.

The count is, of course, 0–0 before the pitcher makes his initial delivery to any hitter. After one pitch, it will be either 0 and 1 or 1 and 0, read and articulated, please, as "oh 'n one" or "one 'n oh," meaning no balls and one strike or no strikes and one ball. Note that the number of balls is always given first, even if there are none.

At 0 and 1 the pitcher is ahead. At 1 and 1, the count evens. At 2 and 1 the batter is ahead. At 2 and 2 the count is even once more. If the count goes to 3 and 2, it is always described as "full"—meaning that any further change in the count will change the situation of the batter: he will either walk, strike out, be out on a play in the field, or be on base. Note that until a batter has two strikes, every foul ball he hits (that isn't

* And for me.

caught) is a strike; but if he has two strikes, he can foul off an unlimited number of pitches and the count will remain unchanged—a situation described as "the count holds."

13. PITCHING POSITION

Every pitch begins with the pitcher placing his right foot (in the case of a right-handed hurler; left for a southpaw) on the rubber, his body facing squarely toward the plate. The classic pitching form is the "full windup." First there is a sequence of rocking (or pumping, as it is sometimes called) motions in which both arms are moved in tandem first in front and then behind the body. If this happens once, the pitcher has pumped once. Again, and he has pumped twice. More pumps than that are usually done to spite the batter.

After pumping once or twice—or simply holding the ball at his waist—the pitcher can pursue any natural movements that will culminate in his throwing the ball. The pivot foot—the foot on the rubber—must remain in contact with the rubber until the ball is released. And he shall, in the language of the rules, "not raise either foot from the ground, except that in his actual delivery of the ball to the batter he may take one step backward and one step forward with his free foot." His free foot being, naturally, the one not toed to the rubber.

Obviously a pitcher who assumed this posture on the mound with a runner on first base would be inviting the runner to steal. So with men on base—excepting a single runner on third, or with the bases loaded, or when the steal of a base is of no importance—the pitcher assumes his "set position." Without a laboriously explicit and somewhat windy explanation, it suffices to say that the set position allows the pitcher to stand sideways on the mound. He must still keep his pivot foot in contact with the rubber, but now it is laterally upon it. And he must come to a complete stop, holding the ball at his waist. This pause, a suspension in the pitching action, can be part of a "stretch," a motion in which the arms are extended over the head and then brought to the waist. Stretch or not, the pitcher must come to a complete stop before delivering the ball.

Now, from the set position—standing sideways, pivot foot on the rubber—once the pitcher goes into his natural motion he is committed to making his pitch without alteration or interruption. Failure to do so results in a balk. While in the set position, but before he goes into pitching motion, he can throw to a base, "step off" the rubber, or pitch. If he steps off, the whole cycle of possibilities occurs once more when he reassumes the set position.

Until quite recently all pitchers used a full windup except when there were men on base. Now, however, a number of pitchers use a no-windup delivery, which begins, correctly and logically, with the same posture as the windup—toe on the rubber, pitcher facing toward the plate—but without the rocking action.*

---

* There are some rather esoteric arguments over which is the preferred motion, windup or no windup. The fundamentals of pitching certainly include these precepts: mastery of three basic pitches—fast ball, curve or slider, change of pace. For mastery, read control—the ability to make the pitch go where the pitcher wants it. Rhythm is also part of pitching. No pianist ever plays a piece of music exactly the same way another pianist does. Pitching is every bit as in-

Sound complicated? Don't you believe it. Baseball is rather like a complex recipe that frightens away many people before they have an opportunity to taste it. But the ingredients go together understandably and logically. Watch a pitcher go into his windup, or pitch from the set position, and the confusion of verbal descriptions is instantly clarified.

14. PITCHING STYLES

And now, friends, for some of the finer points. The pitcher's delivery can refer to the kind of pitch he throws (delivers) or the arm motion used to throw the ball plateward.

In the overhand delivery the arm rises in a full arc above the head and is close to the body. In three-quarter overhand the arm does not rise quite so far and has more lateral movement. Overhand is the most common delivery, owing its popularity to the added leverage it gives to a fast ball and the general benefits it bestows on control. Overhand is sometimes called "coming over the top."

"Sidearm" describes the motion of the arm extended away from the body, more or less parallel to the ground. This is a very difficult delivery for batters of the same handedness as the pitcher to hit. However, it is perhaps easier for dissimilar-handed hitters—left-handed hitters against a right-handed pitcher, for instance—because the batter gets to see the ball a trifle longer.

---

dividualistic. And in the same way the pianist sways to the rhythm of his playing, so the pitcher can feel when he is right. For some pitchers, a windup is helpful in finding that rhythm. For others, it is a hindrance.

A "submarine" delivery is the opposite of over-hand. The knuckles of the pitching hand seem to scrape the top of the mound. It is the least natural motion and the most difficult to control. Only a handful of pitchers are submariners, and perhaps the infrequency with which hitters confront this motion helps to make it more effective.

The next time—or the first time—you watch a pitcher deliver the ball, notice what happens to him after he completes his pitching motion. To a greater or lesser degree, he tends to fall off the mound. This is because his follow-through pulls him off the mound, his body following the direction in which his arm is moving.

15. THE PITCHER AS FIELDER

A pitcher is also a fielder. Or he should be, anyway. A good follow-through should result in his being more or less balanced on both feet so that he can move to his left or right to field a bunt or to stab a ball headed through the box—back over the mound and, presumably, over second base and into center field. On this subject I will say nothing more—except that Robert's follow-through is not the best-looking in the major leagues.* I guess form doesn't always follow function, though. Robert has won the Rawlings Gold Glove–Sporting News All-Star Fielding Team Award four times.

* A harsh but fair judgment. A good fielding pitcher is a "fifth fielder" who can help himself and his team. But the natural or unnatural movements involved in the follow-through can only be improved by changing the pitcher's motion—his pitching fingerprint as it were. The risk of diminishing his pitching excellence (as a result of tampering with his motion) to improve his fielding position simply cannot be justified. Most certainly not at my age.

Good follow-through or bad, a pitcher has several fielding responsibilities. On anything hit to the right side, the pitcher must cover first base. This allows the first baseman to go deep in the hole and throw to the pitcher for the out. To gain this added defensive coverage the pitcher must waste no time getting off the mound. On certain other plays the pitcher must back up third base so that should the expected throw from the outfield be wide of the mark, the runner will be prevented from scoring. With a runner on third, in the event of a wild pitch or a passed ball, the pitcher must rush to the plate so that if the ball is retrieved by the catcher an attempt can be made to nip the runner at the plate.

The Catcher

At the beginning of this chapter it was announced that the battery consisted of two players, the pitcher and the catcher. I think I detect a rumbling in the background that suggests that the catchers' union—and most especially their wives—is demanding equal time. And the catchers deserve it.

1. EQUIPMENT

The equipment that catchers wear—mask, chest-protector, shinguards—is sometimes called "the tools of ignorance." No one seems quite sure who coined this opprobrious term, and though you may hear it occasionally used today, it is uttered more in respect than in assassination. The catcher has the toughest job in baseball. His is the greatest peril from injury—from foul tips, from runners sliding into home, or from tumbling down dugout steps in pursuit of just-out-of-reach foul flies. Yet he must also participate in the cerebrations of pitching—the choice of what pitch is thrown, and where. So, although there is only one arm hurling against the hitter, two heads are pitted against him.

2. SIGNS

This collusion can be carried on in two ways. The first is through the catcher's signs, a code in which the extended fingers of his ungloved hand correspond to certain pitches—one finger usually meaning fast ball, two fingers for curve, and so on. Baseball lore says that the catcher gives the sign, the pitcher takes his sign. If the pitcher disagrees with the catcher's signal, "he shakes him off."

Why can't the batter look at the signs? Well, the catcher is behind him. Moreover, the catcher is in a crouch, and the finger-wriggling takes place in the hollow of his groin, shielded by his thighs. I suppose the batter could crane around and peer down at the catcher. However, he would run the risk of not being set and ready for the pitch. Also, he would be subject to a certain amount of ridicule. So no peeking is the standard practice.

The alternate method of communication is more prosaic. The catcher simply trots out to the mound and talks with the pitcher about the series of pitches they will toss at the batter. Normally, these missions to the mound are concluded by the catcher giving the pitcher an encouraging pat on the rump. In fact, whenever anybody goes out to the mound to talk to the pitcher—the manager, an infielder, or the catcher—the meeting always breaks up with a pat on the pitcher's lower back.

Back to the serious business of catching. In addition to calling for certain specific kinds of pitches, the catcher may also indicate where they should be thrown. He does this by positioning his glove—in baseballese he "sets his target," inside or outside, high or low.

3. THE TARGET

The terms "inside" and "outside" are a trifle imprecise. "Inside" can refer to the inside portion of the plate, the half of the plate nearest the batter, or the inside corner. But "inside" can also mean that a certain pitch is a ball. Similarly, "outside" can mean the outside half of the plate, the outside corner, or outside for a ball.

Two other directional terms of somewhat greater accuracy are "tight" and "away." A tight pitch is not, contrary to first impression, one that has been dipped in bourbon; it is a pitch close to the batter. Two other expressions that refer to pitching close to the batter are "keeping the ball in on him"— close to him—and the more colorful "jamming him." In pitching parlance, to jam is to "keep the ball on the batter's fists," where, if the batter does hit it, contact will be made only with the thinnest portion of the bat, the handle, and the ball will be weakly driven.

"Away" means the obvious: away from the hitter. But the word has shades of meaning. For example, if somebody says, "He missed outside with a fast ball," he clearly means that the fast ball was off, not on, the outside corner of the plate and the umpire called it a ball. The pitch was away, right? Technically yes, semantically no. "Away" is more of an objective than a directive, as when a pitcher says, "He's a dead pull hitter so I tried to keep the ball away from him."

In this (more usual) usage, "away" means away from the hitter's strength, regardless of whether the pitch referred to was a ball or a strike.

The catcher has always seemed to me to be both heroic and stoic. As already indicated, he absorbs more physical punishment than any other player. That's heroic. But he also spends much of his playing time in a crouching position that I couldn't endure for nine minutes, let alone nine innings. That's stoic.

4. CALLING THE PITCH

Although the pitcher and catcher are a team within a team—one is the battery mate of the other—their relationship is a shifting one, depending upon their experience. When a rookie or an inexperienced pitcher is throwing to a veteran catcher, it is the latter who literally "calls the game": tells the pitcher what to throw on almost every pitch. Thus, when a young pitcher wins, he will often credit the catcher with calling a great game. On the other hand, if the pitcher is a veteran, he will take command. The crucial element here is knowing the strengths and weaknesses of each batter in the opposing lineup, something which comes mostly from experience and from "the book." This isn't something you borrow from the library. It is the sum of all that everyone on the team knows—and especially the pooled knowledge of the pitchers, the catchers, the coaches, and the manager—about how to pitch to each opposing hitter.

Before the game, the team assembles in the clubhouse and a general defensive strategy meeting is held. At this meeting the infielders and outfielders are reminded that Smith hits to left and left center and occasionally down the line in right, but never to right center. The infielders are cautioned to guard against the possibility of a bunt by Jones, who over the last few games has tried this stratagem several times. And the pitcher for that game and probably the relief pitchers who will be in the bullpen discuss who has been having good luck against batter Brown and what pitch has recently been used to get him out. The battery also weighs the likelihood of various hitters stealing once they reach base.

5. HOLDING THE RUNNER
It is the pitcher's job to keep the runner close, preventing him from taking a big (long) lead which increases the likelihood of the attempted steal becoming a successful steal. It is a baseball adage that most bases are stolen off the pitcher. For no matter how powerful the catcher's throwing arm, if the pitcher allows the runner to get a good jump (as applied to his lead away from a base, not a fly ball) it will be almost impossible to throw him out.

We have seen that in a situation with runners on base in which a steal is likely, the pitcher throws from his set position, not his windup. In the case of a right-handed pitcher, before throwing to the plate he will peer over his shoulder at the runner on first. This could be an ocular bluff to force the runner to shorten his lead. Or it could be the prelude to a pickoff throw. (A left-handed pitcher has a distinct advantage in such a situation, since he is facing first base and need not whirl before throwing to first. With a runner on third, the advantage is reversed. Now the right-hander faces the baserunner, and it is the southpaw who must peek over his shoulder.) The pitcher's attempt to catch the runner before he can return to first (or second or third, for that matter) is often called his "move," as in "Whitey Ford of the Yankees had a great move to first." But the runner is referred to as having been "picked off."

With a runner on first, sometimes the catcher will throw there after a pitch to the batter. This is called a pickoff throw. And on occasion, if the catcher thinks the baserunner will be trying to steal on the upcoming pitch—as suggested by the score, or the character of the hitter or the runner—he will signal for a "pitchout." This is a pitch thrown intentionally far beyond (outside) the reach of the batter and at a height enabling the catcher to turn loose his throw with maximum quickness. By definition, a pitchout is always a ball. However, no matter how obviously a pitchout is outside the strike zone, if the batter swings at the pitch while "trying to protect the runner" from being thrown out, the pitch is a strike.

Please read that sentence again. Doesn't it suggest that there is another brand of collusion taking place besides that between the catcher and the pitcher? It suggests precisely that. And sometimes there is—between the batter and the runner at first.

Which brings us to the threshold of our next chapter—the antithesis of the collaborative talents of pitcher and catcher: Hitting.

Hitting

The bat shall be a smooth, rounded stick, not more than two and three-fourths inches in diameter at the thickest part and not more than 42 inches in length. The bat shall be 1) one piece of solid wood, or 2) formed from a block of wood consisting of two or more pieces of wood bonded together with an adhesive in such a way that the grain direction of all pieces is essentially parallel to the length of the bat. Any such laminated bat shall contain only wood or adhesive, except for a clear finish.—*Official Baseball Rules*

The objective of the hitter is to solidly hit a round object, a ball, with a rounded club, a bat. This would seem to be impossible. For talented ball-players with the flawed abilities of mortals it is merely very, very difficult.

The skills of the fielder are partly based on natural ability. But much can be learned, improved, even perfected, by practice. Through diligence, an outfielder can learn to chart the course of a fly ball, can master the technique of cutting off a hit. True, the strength of his throwing arm cannot be improved, but the zealous outfielder can be taught to throw more accurately. And every infielder has become an adequate glove man, or he could not survive in the majors.

The Basics

But for the batter the outlook is less encouraging. Unless he has the basic aptitude, no amount of practice, no number of sessions with a batting coach, *nothing* will enable him to become a really good hitter. But—and there is always, in every aspect of life and no less so in baseball, the paradox which begins with "but"—there is the possibility that he is a good hitter and that various technical factors, things he is doing wrong, are preventing him from realizing his true potential.

Gather round, ladies, and let us strip away the folklore and mystery from the art-science-mystique of hitting.

Let us begin by remembering something we have already learned: the role of fear in baseball. Fear is, you will recall, the constant companion of every hitter, a specter of weakness which, at one point or another, every pitcher seeks to lure from the back of the hitter's mind to the front. This fear of being hit must be repressed, or suppressed, or otherwise banished from consciousness. For the act of hitting begins by stepping *into* the pitch. Not literally, of course, but almost.

The hitter stands in the batter's box. As the pitcher delivers, he must make up his mind to swing—or, just as important, not to swing—in an instant.* Of course, in order to hit the ball he must begin his swing before the ball reaches the plate. Now, in order to do more than just

* Actually, a little less than an instant. A good major-league fast ball is traveling at somewhere in the neighborhood of 100 miles per hour. Facing that speed, the batter has about half a second in which to make up his mind. Personally, I think even that's too darn long.

weakly tap the ball he must step into the pitch. Thus the batter's rear foot—his right foot if he is hitting right-handed, his left foot if he's a lefty swinger—is planted firmly on the ground. With his front foot, he strides forward.

Moving up from ground level, the next (and most obvious) element in hitting is the batter's swing. A good swing should be level. Or maybe not. (If your husband just happens to be reading over your shoulder he will, at this point, mutter, "What does she know?" and go back to reading the sports page.) A level swing is, when you think about it, good only when the pitch is level too. And most pitches are not on the level—a pardonable pun. What is really meant by a level swing is that the arc through which the bat must travel to hit a pitch solidly—whether that pitch is high or low—must be smooth. But except where it is meeting a waist-high pitch, the bat really travels in a flattened parabola.

Many good hitters got that way by learning to hit down on the ball. Hitting down, also called tomahawking, sacrifices distance for maximum velocity within the infield and the closer reaches of the outfield. Hitting down results in hard ground balls, the "smashes" so beloved by broadcasters, and in line drives—"frozen ropes," the ballplayers call them—to the outfield.

If you watch a hitter through binoculars or on television, you will note that not all good hitters are powerful men. Even our most prodigious home-run hitters are not necessarily the fulfillment of a Charles Atlas promotion. It is true that such hitters as Frank Howard (6 feet, 7 inches; 270 pounds) and Willie McCovey (6 feet, 4 inches; 200 pounds) are big men. Your husband, if he has returned to argue—which is, after baseball itself, the fan's most delicious delight—may mention Ted Kluszewski, of the Cincinnati Reds, and Gil Hodges of the Brooklyn/Los Angeles Dodgers, now manager of the New York Mets. Both these gentlemen were very, very strong—Mr. Kluszewski, in fact, having to slice the sleeves of his jersey in order to accommodate his biceps. (And both were, interestingly enough, quiet gentlemen on the field. Perhaps they had nothing to prove through needlessly aggressive behavior.)

The Swing
But the power of the swing is not necessarily derived from the shoulders or arms. It can come from the wrists. A gifted hitter can, with a snap of his wrists, flick the bat swiftly and with enormous power. Willie Mays, perhaps the greatest ballplayer of the last several decades, second only to the incomparable Babe Ruth in the home-run derby, is a wrist hitter. So was Ted Williams.* The

---

* Unconsciously, my wife has reflected a prejudice that is endemic among today's baseball fans, and even among the players. I refer to the corruption of "home-run hitter" into "good hitter." Fans are enraptured by homers because they are dramatic. Certainly there is an expectancy when a slugger is at the plate. The pitcher knows that this batter is more likely to hit a homer than most batters, and he bears down, concentrates on his pitching with a special intensity and forgoes the luxury of pacing himself, of conserving his energy. But home-run hitters do something else besides hit a lot of home runs. They strike out. The big swing sacrifices a small but important quotient of control. The hitter is bent on overpowering the ball, not on simply meeting it squarely. Why this emphasis on home runs? Simple. Ballplayers say, "Home-run hitters drive Cadillacs," meaning that the guy who is a

wrist hitter can wait a fraction of a second longer than the hitter whose power is derived from shoulders and arms. This gives him more time to discern what kind of pitch is on its way, and where—inside or out, high or low.

What else are good hitters made of? They are often men of vision, which is to say they must have phenomenal eyesight. They must have, or have developed, a great sense of timing, the partly learned but mostly instinctive combination of reflexes that enables a batter to connect with the ball. They must believe in themselves. And they must have desire.

The Mental Side

A hitter must think positively. He must have a certain swagger, a sense of invincibility, of inevitable triumph in his personal battle with the pitcher. Moreover, he must maintain this convic-

---

renowned slugger makes more money than the hitter who hits for a higher batting average but fewer homers. One other thing that this added emphasis on home runs has accomplished is the near extinction of the really fine non-home-run hitter. Hitters who have no business trying to hit home runs are doing so, with the result that their batting averages are fearsomely eroded. There are, I promise you, a lot of .230 hitters who would be much closer to .300 if they stopped swinging for the fences. Mind you, as a pitcher I'm not complaining. But as a fan—and I am one—it seems a shame to see ballplayers vainly pursuing a goal they have no hope of reaching and simultaneously ignoring the chance to allow their hitting talents to mature naturally. By the way, not all the great home-run hitters have been wrist hitters. Babe Ruth's power was generated from every ounce of his enormous physique, and particularly by his powerful arms.

tion at bat even though he knows that the majority of the time he will not be the victor.* However, a hitter must keep his confidence within bounds. He cannot allow himself to be seduced by his ego into an attitude of sneering disdain for the pitcher. Overconfidence can be as deadly as insecurity.

Discipline

In many ways, the good hitter is a disciplined hitter. Every hitter has a weakness. Perhaps he is least effective when hitting low inside curves, or fast balls outside. After a while word gets around among the pitchers. But such is the personal balance of the duel between pitcher and batter that the pitching gospel which says that Tom Smith has trouble with pitches low and away also tells Mr. Smith that in certain situations he can expect to see a pitch low and away— with the count 1 and 1, or 1 and 2, for example.

* Proof of this is the player's batting average. An at-bat is an official time at bat, an opportunity for the batter to get a hit. It is not an official time at bat when a player walks; when he sacrifices (*intentionally* makes an out himself but succeeds in moving a baserunner from first to second or second to third, usually by bunting—a sacrifice bunt); when he hits a sacrifice fly on which a run scores; when he is hit by a pitch or is awarded first base because of interference by the catcher. A hit, then, is any ball so struck that the batter reaches first base safely without the help of an error by a fielder. For the purposes of computing a batting average, every hit, whether a single, double, triple, or home run, counts as one. The arithmetic consists of dividing the total number of hits by the batter's total number of official at-bats to three decimal places. Thus, if a player has 30 hits in 100 official times at bat his batting average is .300.

In such situations Mr. Smith prepares himself for the pitch that is supposed to be especially difficult for him. This kind of intelligent analysis of a hitter's own weakness can be of inestimable help to him. Meanwhile, a smart pitcher will reason: "Just because Smith *is* a thinking hitter he will expect to be pitched low and away in this situation, so I'll pitch low and inside." And thus the game of counter-thinking continues.

Notice that I refer to the analysis of what pitch the hitter expects to see as "thinking." Hitters are often slandered by being accused of guessing. "Smith was completely fooled by the curve. He was guessing and expected a fast ball." (You will not infrequently hear that a pitcher kept them guessing.) To a greater or less degree, all hitters guess about the next pitch. If they're right, we call the process "thinking"; if they're wrong, "guessing."

Back to discipline. Besides enabling a hitter honestly to recognize his weakness—which, we can presume, will sooner or later become clear to the pitcher—discipline is a potent hitting catalyst in other ways. First, discipline is obviously involved in the self-restraint which enables a batter to lay off a bad pitch—to take the pitch. This is the obverse side of hitting's golden coin which bears the inscription: Get a good pitch to hit.

Bad pitches are not guilty of moral turpitude. They are simply pitches that are out of the strike zone, or they are pitches which are not the hitter's preferred pitch. By elimination, a good pitch to hit is probably a strike, or it is a pitch of the kind, and in the position, which the batter likes.

For almost every hitter, and certainly for every

slugger, the good pitch is one over the inside part of the plate, belt high or higher. What's so good about this? Well, it is the easiest kind of pitch to pull. You probably recall from earlier chapters that the shortest distance between the plate and the stands is down the line, and that a batter's strength—his ability to pull the ball— is universally to the side of the plate from which he bats. Hence, high inside pitches have a tendency to wind up in an exultant fan's grasp while an equally exultant hitter trots around the bases.

The same mental discipline that prevents a batter from swinging at bad balls also keeps him abreast of what kind of hit he should try for. The first objective of a hitter is to get on base. Hence the hallowed observation that "a walk's as good as a hit." However, if you are a good hitter and come up in a situation in which a man is on second and there are two out, your disciplined mind will tell you that it isn't a walk that's needed but a hit. The same mind will also reason that an outfield single that normally scores a runner from second is the minimum requirement.

Why should the batter think of a single, rather than a home run? Well, because a single can be stroked with shorter bat swing, one more easily controlled, than the big swing which powers a home run.

Well then, you ask, how is it that anybody ever hits a home run with men on base? Shouldn't the hits in such situations normally be singles? That's a good question, and I'm sorry I got you to ask it. Perhaps the answer lies in one of many possibilities. Not all hitters feel they can adjust their swing. A true home-run hitter has a potential which is rare, and to sacrifice that maximum potential for a tactical situation may be, illogical as it sounds, a poor decision. The likelihood of the hitter smacking a homer has to be measured against the effect on his hitting of a change in the pattern of his swing.

Since these comments on hitting contain so many qualified statements, so many exceptions that the original statement seems to have been modified to a point of thoroughly diminished authority, you can see why hitting is the subject of heated debate.

A final example of the exception-that-proves-the-rule confusion: even though hitters should wait for good pitches, there are some who are particularly adroit at hitting bad pitches. Such successful rule-breakers are called bad-ball hitters.*

---

* One notorious bad-ball hitter was Joe "Ducky" Medwick, who used to play with the Cardinals. There is a (perhaps apocryphal) story about Medwick that reveals both his facility at hitting bad balls and the quandary of the manager or batting coach when confronted with a player who can successfully do what he shouldn't. Medwick's manager had warned Ducky he would fine him $100 for swinging at bad balls. Ducky came to bat in the ninth inning. The bases were loaded, two men were out, and the Cardinals were trailing by one run. Medwick worked the count to 3 and 2. Remember that if Medwick were to walk he would force in the runner from third, there being, as the saying goes, no place to put him. And remember too that the Cards desperately needed the tying run. At any rate, the pitcher delivered, a pitch way over the top of Medwick's head—or it would have been. Medwick swung—he almost had to jump high in the air to reach the ball—and somehow managed to slam

The Stance

We should not neglect the batter's feet at the plate. Although the word "stance" applies to the batter's total posture, it is often used to describe only the position of his feet. In the classic stance, the feet are parallel. This is sometimes called a straightaway stance. Most hitters deviate from this position either a little or a lot. If the lead foot, the one closest to the pitcher, is angled away from the rear foot (toward third base for a right-handed hitter; first base for a left-handed hitter), the stance is described as "open." In this position, the batter has his body partly turned toward the pitcher. Therefore he can watch the incoming pitch a trifle more comfortably than from the straightaway position, which requires him to peek over his shoulder, or to drop his shoulder. The open stance also lets the batter pull the ball— or forces him to. He has excellent bat position for a pitch thrown inside, but he sacrifices his ability to hit outside pitches. In fact, to hit an outside curve he may have to lunge at the ball, which is hardly likely to result in a controlled swing or in hitting to all fields.

What's the alternative to an open stance? You guessed it: a closed stance. Now the left foot of the right-handed hitter (the right foot of the left-handed hitter) is closer to the plate than is the rear foot. What advantage does the closed stance boast? It provides good bat coverage across the full width of the plate, enabling the batter to

---

the ball into the stands for a home run. The fans broke into cheers, and Medwick was smiling happily as he crossed home plate and received the congratulations of his teammates. "Congratulations, Ducky," said his manager. "That'll cost you a hundred bucks."

hit both inside and outside pitches with authority. Also, it tends to help him hit to all fields—to right, left, and center. This in turn presupposes a willingness on the part of the hitter to go "with the pitch" and not try to pull every ball at which he swings. However, just to confuse matters further, a good wrist hitter *can* pull the ball from a closed stance because he has a quick bat and can get around on even an inside fast ball.

For the most part, a hitter's stance is a matter of personal idiosyncrasy—of style, comfort, habit. But a batting coach may suggest that a hitter change his stance to compensate for a defect or weakness that pitchers have discerned and are exploiting. For example, some hitters have trouble with curve balls because of "overstriding." That is, the batter sees the pitch coming and decides it is a curve. He times the break of the curve and takes a half-stride, hesitates, and then commits himself too late by taking another stride. To prevent overstriding, a hitter may adopt a spread stance. In this case the body assumes an inverted Y shape, with the feet spread wide apart. Obviously this position discourages the batter from striding prematurely by severely limiting his ability to step into the pitch.*

* Another way for a batter to compensate for the curve ball's change in direction is to change his position at the plate. If he stands in the forward part of the box he has a good chance to catch the curve before it breaks. By doing so, though, he shortens the amount of time available to him to decide what kind of a pitch is coming, and its direction. Even more frequently, batters will stand deep in the box. Although this does nothing to ameliorate the directional change of a breaking pitch, it does give the batter the maximum interval to follow the ball after it leaves the pitcher's

I have always been fascinated by the ritual which every hitter practices at the plate. It begins when he is kneeling in the on-deck circle, or standing and swinging a leaded bat—so that the real one he finally uses will feel comparatively light. (Apparently even though the brain knows what's going on, the muscles are nonetheless fooled.) Then he marches up to the plate, tossing aside the leaded bat with casual unconcern. He pauses for a moment and rubs dirt on his hands, or perhaps he uses the batter's resin bag. (In both cases he is trying to make his hands sticky so that he will have a firm grip on the bat.) Adroitly he knocks excess dirt from his spikes with his bat. He may glare out at the mound, or perhaps not. In any case, he aggressively steps into the batter's box and smooths the dirt which has been harrowed by the previous batter's spikes. Having thus completed his groundskeeping chores, he assumes his stance. Often that assumption begins by digging a hole for his rear foot, the one that will bear most of his weight until he strides.*

---

hand and to decide whether he wants to swing or not. Needless to say, both of these alternatives are widely known and used—or I should not be able to discuss them. For—who knows?—there may be a hitter in the audience.

 * There was a time in the major leagues when the sight of a hitter digging in was seen as a gross insult by the pitching brethren. Almost certainly the immediate response was a brushback pitch. However, with the passage of time we all grow in understanding. I would say that a hitter who obviously carves a niche for his rear foot can now expect to be brushed back no more than half the time. The reasoning here is simple: all hitters need stability of body to swing with authority. The rear foot must be firmly planted to ob-

Finally, the hitter is set. As a final flourish, he pumps the bat a few times, taking short, sharp swings. This isn't done to intimidate the pitcher; he is rediscovering his feeling of all being right at the plate, much as you and I have to reposition the rear-view mirror when we climb into the family car after hubby's been using it, and, having done that, squirm around a bit to make sure that we're comfortable.

Thinking at the Plate
Even given the right physical equipment—eyes, muscles, reflexes, timing—a hitter can realize his full potential only with constant practice. And during the game he must be as ready mentally as he is physically. He must be aware of who is pitching and what pitch is likely to be thrown. This last consideration is based not only on what the tactical situation is—whether there are runners on base, how many outs, who is the next batter—but also on the dimensions of the ball park, and weather. Is the wind blowing in or out? Is it a dark day or, if the game is played at night, how effective are the lights? Is it early in the game or late, and what is the score? In a close game the pitcher won't take a chance (maybe); if he enjoys a big lead, he may. And, of course, there is the ball-and-strike count.

It may be repetitious, but it bears repeating: baseball is a supremely tactical game, of considerable subtlety and occasional cunning. What

---

tain that stability. Thus, digging in is a threat to the pitcher. So if the hitter is sending up dirt like a tunneling mole, he is more likely to be forced to bail out in a hurry than if he is more discreet in his earth-moving.

you see is often simply the visible evidence of plot and counterplot—although, as we shall see in a later chapter, a good deal of the strategic maneuvering can be seen and understood, if you know not only what is happening but why.

The count concerns us because it affects the hitter by denying him certain choices. Once the pitcher has two strikes, the batter is forced to protect the plate. He can't afford to take a pitch that is questionably close to being a (third) strike. This is one reason why a batter often hits a disproportionately high number of foul balls with two strikes; he is chopping at pitches he might have taken with only one strike. To help him protect the plate, the batter may shorten his swing by choking up on the bat. The act is far less violent than it sounds. No one is throttled. It simply means that the batter moves his hands up the bat a couple of inches away from the end, resulting in a shortened swing that is easier to control.*

* It should be noted that hitters who have no vainglorious ambitions to be sluggers may always choke up on the bat. The lead-off hitter—the first of the nine players on the team to come to bat—may always choke up on the bat. One of the reasons he *is* batting first is that he gets on base a lot, probably as a result of singles and also walks. Why mostly singles? Chances are if he had more power he would be batting somewhat later, in order to drive in other runners. The logic expressed here is admittedly simplistic, but it does have considerable basis in fact. Pitchers also choke up on the bat, mostly because they are poor hitters and the sacrifice of power for bat-control is for them an academic loss. Please note that to choke up on the bat (or, as it is variously said, to choke up on the handle) is a well-mannered baseball idiom. Not

Bat-Control

If the home-run slugger stands as the hitting idol
of the fans, the batter who has bat-control is even
more admired by the players themselves. I hasten
to add that there is nothing common about being
able to hit home runs. But the hitter who can
manipulate his bat is even rarer. Moreover, the
finesse with which a batter "hits 'em where they
ain't" is too often lost on the fan, who equates
power with skill.

Really to handle a bat, a hitter must be able
to stroke the ball to either the left or right side
of the diamond at will. This is an extremely valu-
able skill. Advancing a runner from first to second,
where he can score on a single, or from second
to third, where, with fewer than two out, he can
score on a sacrifice fly, is at the heart of baseball
strategy.*

---

so the verb "to choke." This refers to a player, a team,
or even an umpire who surrenders to pressure and
does not perform up to expectations. A player who
disputes an umpire's decision can tear off his hat and
jump on it. He can snarl at the ump, even indulge in
a brief flurry of colorful language. But if he accuses
the umpire of choking up, the player will find himself
out of the game faster than you can say "nearsighted,
pigheaded arbiter." To say that someone chokes, then,
is the supreme baseball insult.

 * Literally, the batter sacrifices himself by hitting a
fly ball on which the runner is able to score after the
catch. Remember that the runner cannot advance
from third base—or any base, for that matter—until
the ball is caught. If he does, and the team in the field
notices his premature departure, and a fielder touches
the bag while holding the ball—an act always accompanied by piteous screams of "He left early"—the
umpire will declare him out. In baseballese, this is
called an appeal play.

The Hit-and-Run

One way of accomplishing the advancement of the runner from first to second is by "playing hit-and-run." This means that the manager signals (in a way to be explored a bit later) both the batter and the runner that on the next pitch the hit-and-run is on. To the runner, this means he must break for second as soon as the pitcher begins his motion. To the batter, it means that he must make contact with the ball, trying to hit a ground ball *behind* the runner, to the right side of the infield. The theory here is that the runner will then be so close to second that he cannot be caught in a double play. Of course, if the batter hits a line drive that is caught by an infielder, the runner on first will be doubled up unless he manages to scurry back to the bag ahead of the throw.

Suppose that the hitter has mastered the art of bat-control. The signal is flashed: hit-and-run on the next pitch. The pitcher goes into his motion, and simultaneously the runner on first breaks for second. The infielders are probably unaware of the hit-and-run. They must assume that the runner is attempting to steal. And either the shortstop or second baseman will sprint over to cover the bag.

Now, as the pitcher's delivery moves toward the plate, the hitter notices out of the corner of his eye which infielder is moving over to cover the bag. And such is his control of the bat that he will attempt—often with success—to hit the ball through the space vacated by that fielder. If the shortstop scoots over to second, the hitter will try to smack a ground ball through short; if the second baseman covers, the hitter will poke the ball to the right side.

Sometimes the defense smells out the play and suspects that the hit-and-run is on. If so, the catcher will call for a pitchout. Then the hitter will try to protect the runner by lunging for the ball, even though it is far outside. He may even fling his bat at the ball in order to foul off the pitch and prevent the imminent possibility of the runner being thrown out at second.

Getting to First Base

The final element in hitting is the follow-through, the after-contact form of the hitter. After the bat strikes the ball, the bat should continue around in a relatively smooth course, and the body, particularly the torso, should be twisted in a powerful but regular sequence. Clearly, a batter who gets tangled up in his own feet after hitting the ball is losing precious time in leaving the batter's box—time that can make the difference between an infield single and an out, or a long outfield single and a double.

As a matter of fact, the speed with which a batter gets down the line to first can be instrumental in raising his batting average several points. Not only will he beat out a hit on a play in which a slower batter would have been out, but, because he is fast afoot, the infielders will have to play up a couple of steps, thus increasing the likelihood that ground balls which normally would be outs will shoot past the tightened infield.

In the race to get to first base, the left-handed batter has an obvious advantage. Just because he bats from the left side of the plate, he is a couple of feet closer to first than is the right-handed batter. This may seem like a mere token advantage. It isn't. A running stride can easily be the difference between a rally-starting hit and a rally-ending out. Increasingly, as a matter of fact, a ballplayer's speed is being recognized as one of the principal determinants of winning baseball. Interestingly enough, the fastest man at, say, the fifty-yard dash is not necessarily the fastest man at the thirty-yard dash—getting down the 90 feet of basepath. Acceleration is very important in getting to first base: getting out of the batter's box swiftly and getting up to maximum speed in the shortest possible time.

Now let's discuss the man who puts all the offense and defense together: the manager.

The Manager

The Manager is a person appointed by the club to be responsible for the team's actions on the field, and to represent the team in communications with the umpire and the opposing team. A player may be appointed manager.—*Official Baseball Rules*

So sayeth the rule book. And the rule book is never wrong—perhaps. A simple, straightforward description of a simple job, one that anyone could do. (Ask any fan and he will certainly tell you that *he* could do it for his favorite team, and better than the guy who's managing now, too!) Maybe so.

And maybe not.

The Manager's Responsibilities

Here, not quite selected at random—but certainly in no particular order—is a partial catalogue of a manager's responsibilities. He selects the players who will at least begin playing the game; he has a strong voice in deciding whether his club should make a trade with another team; he must render decisions throughout the game (should the hitter take or hit away? should the pitcher stay in or be relieved, and if so, by whom?); he must be able to handle the disparate personalities among the twenty-five players on his team; he must get the most out of his veterans and also carefully bring to maturity the raw talent of the rookies; he must be able to handle sportswriters' questions, some of which may be rude, stupid, or purposefully calculated to make him lose his temper; he must teach those players who need teaching, even though they feel they do not; he must inspire his team with confidence that he himself may not feel at all; he must arbitrate petty squabbles and mete out justice by levying fines as punishment for breaches of discipline; he must win, though ultimately there is only one pennant to be had in each league, and only one team will emerge victorious from the World Series. And he must keep his job.

On a daily basis, the manager's duties most obviously begin by filling in the lineup card. This is a printed form with spaces on which the manager can enter the names and positions of the nine players he selects to start the game. Various factors will affect his choice, principally whether the opposing pitcher is right-handed or left-handed, for many right-handed hitters are most effective against southpaws, while many lefty swingers can hit only right-handed pitchers. The order in which the selected names appear on the lineup card is also the order in which the players will come to bat.

Even though eight of the nine names on the lineup card may be the same day after day—for certainly the same pitcher's name will appear only once every four or five days—the lineup card must be thoughtfully considered prior to every game. The manager has established a pitching rotation so that his four best starting pitchers are scheduled to work with at least three days' rest between starts. So the pitcher's name is generally the first one the manager puts down, and he puts it in ninth place in the batting order. There are two reasons for this. First, pitchers are usually, we have discovered, weak hitters, and in the ninth position they come to bat as infrequently as possible. The second reason is that the top of the order—the batters hitting first, second, and third—will bat behind (after) the pitcher. In later innings they may be scheduled to hit in the same inning: pitcher, leadoff, number-two hitter. And it is at this point that a pinch-hitter can most effectively be inserted in the lineup.*

In the best of all managerial worlds, let's see how the characteristics of different players commend them to different slots in the batting order.

1. THE BATTING ORDER
Batting in the number-one position is the leadoff man. It is guaranteed that the leadoff will indeed lead off in only one inning, the first. But the sequential logic reflected in the lineup remains the same even if the leadoff man comes up for his second at-bat with one out, or even two out. Also, the first inning is important because

* In baseballese and, derivatively, elsewhere, "pinch" means in place of, substituted for. Thus a pinch-hitter is one who comes off the bench and bats in place of another hitter. In the same way, a pinch-runner is a speedy player who is substituted for a slow-footed base-runner. Note that once a player has been taken out of the game, he cannot re-enter it under any circumstances. However, a pinch-hitter can remain in the game if the manager so chooses, but only in place of some player who is taken out of the game. The player who was pinch-hit *for* is gone until the next game.

it is the first opportunity to score. And the team that scores first, as we shall see, enjoys the luxury of taking a few chances, while the team that trails can hardly afford the risk.*

The leadoff man has the task of getting on base. He has a good eye at the plate, enabling him to collect lots of walks. He won't hit with power, but he will have excellent speed and be a good baserunner.

The second batter should be adept at bunting, hit-and-run, and other tactics which advance the runner. Both the leadoff man and the number-two batter should be good hitters; otherwise they will have little opportunity to practice their tandem offensive techniques.

The number-three hitter is traditionally the best hitter on the team. He will have a high batting average and also hit with power. If the first two hitters have done their job, there will be at least one runner on base for him to drive in. And if not, he will at least have a chance to come to the plate.

The number-four hitter is a slugger, probably the best home-run hitter on the team. The reason, as you have already figured out, is that if there are runners on base in advance of the slugger, and he does sock a homer, these runners will score

* The generalization is true, but perhaps a trifle compressed. The advantage of being ahead—with its converse freedom to take chances which are simultaneously denied to the team behind—increases with every passing inning. A three-run lead in the first inning is good. A three-run lead in the ninth inning—with only one more inning in which the opponents can catch up—is better, by eight innings. The risks are mostly those of aggressive base-running: stealing and the hit-and-run.

in front of him. The number-four hitter in the lineup is reverently referred to as "hitting clean-up": he wipes the bases clean, or tries to.

The number-five and -six hitters are usually power hitters too, though perhaps they do not hit for a high or even respectable average, are slow runners, or are otherwise deficient. Together with the number-four hitter, these hitting positions are sometimes called the "meat" part of the lineup—because, I presume, of the size of the sluggers. Sometimes the term is also applied to the three-through-six slots, depending on how much slugging strength a particular team can boast.

The number-eight hitter (and to some degree the number-seven hitter) certainly suffers from hitting in front of the team's worst hitter, the pitcher. Moreover, seven and eight aren't particularly good hitters to begin with, else they wouldn't be slotted so late in the order. Thus the opposing pitcher can, in certain situations, give them poor pitches to hit, since an almost sure out, the pitcher, is behind them. Conversely, and no less unpleasantly for these hitters, some pitchers try especially hard to get them out, particularly if their being out will end an inning and bring either the number-eight hitter or the pitcher up first in the next inning.*

---

* The pitcher is trying to give himself a cushion for the next inning. To start an inning by pitching to your opposing pitcher is reasonable assurance that the other team will be one-third retired when the leadoff man trudges to the plate. Also, since the top of the order is coming to bat, this is the point at which you can best use the "extra" out. For example, you can give up two singles and get two more outs and end the inning. But if the inning begins with the leadoff man, not the pitcher, you may later have given up two hits and

2. PLATOONING

Most managers do not have the good fortune to be able to assemble a lineup that will man eight positions day after day. Injuries take their toll of available ballplayers during the season. Rarely will a player hit right- and left-handed pitching equally well. In the face of the latter exigency, the manager resorts to "platooning." This means that two players "share" a position, the decision as to which one plays depending on whether a right-hander or southpaw is pitching. The frequent necessity to platoon the ballplayers underlines the value of the switch-hitter, the batter who can hit either right- or left-handed and who simply changes (switches, you see) from one side of the plate to the other when a pitching change occasions it.

Most managers practice their craft according to the book. They play the percentages, opting to follow what years of experience have taught them, sometimes painfully, about when to sacrifice, when to hit away, and so on. Some managers do gamble, but only infrequently. As you might imagine, a manager who tries to catch his opposite number napping cannot attempt the unexpected all the time, lest the unexpected deteriorate, through overuse, into the expected.

3. MANAGERIAL DECISIONS

Although the manager does control the actions of the ballplayers to a great extent, there are at least a couple of occasions when he does not. The first such instance is, of course, when the count is 3 and 2 on the hitter. In such circumstances

gotten two outs—but one more out still remains to be made. Of such calculation is baseball made.

the only exception to the rule that the hitter is on his own occurs when he is woefully weak at hitting. For example, if the pitcher is at bat with the bases loaded and one out, the manager *may* have him take a 3-and-2 pitch, figuring that the worst that can then happen is that the pitch will be called strike three. (But if allowed to swing, he might hit into an inning-ending double play.) If a hitter is an established star, the manager will be inclined to let him hit away with men on base most of the time. And if a runner has proved that he is wondrously effective at stealing bases, he may get the green light to go on any pitch he chooses. But these are exceptions, based on the exceptional ability—or lack of ability—that a ballplayer has displayed during the course of his career.

A player, or a fan steeped in the lore of the game, can make an isolated decision within the context of the game. But it takes a special kind of baseball perspective to think beyond that single decision—to consider, as it were, the echoes of that decision as they will affect the game in later innings. A pinch-hitter used early in the game will not be available to support a ninth-inning rally. A relief pitcher brought in too early may have to be pinch-hit for the next inning, so the necessity to stave off further scoring by the opposition must be weighed against who else is available for relief and whether a rally is actually under way or merely hoped for.

4. THE BENCH
The manager derives much of his tactical mobility from his bench—not the planks in the dugout, but the players, over and above the nine starters,

who sit there. "A deep bench" or "a strong bench" is baseball parlance for reserve strength; a manager who has this is analogous to the fortunate hostess who has a thick file of tested recipes which have proved successful, in contrast to the gal next door who can offer her guests only the one dish she has perfected.

Bench strength is sometimes present simply in the profusion of good ballplayers a team has amassed—not just the necessary three good outfielders, but five, plus another whose poor fielding but heavy hitting relegate him mostly to pinchhitting chores. It can also be present as a result of the versatility of some ballplayers. Consider the utility infielder, victim of a most unprepossessing label. He may not hit as well as the third baseman, or be quite as sharp a fielder as the shortstop or second baseman. But he can play all three positions. In an emergency he may be able to play first base, or even to assume the catching duties. Clearly, the manager who has this kind of multi-position talent has one player who embodies the reserve strength of several positions.*

Every ballplayer wants to play every day. Since

* Two utility players *extraordinaire* are Cesar Tovar of the Minnesota Twins and Cookie Rojas, now, I'm happy to say, a member of the Cardinals. In one game Tovar played one inning at each position—including pitcher! Sure, this was something of a promotional demonstration, but he did it quite well. Rojas has also played all nine positions, but never in the same game. Neither of these gentlemen is a normal utility player, and, in truth, one hesitates to call such amazing versatility by the somewhat deprecating term "utility." Both are semi-regulars, or super-subs, or some such.

a major-league team is permitted to carry twenty-five players, it is obvious that not everyone will play all the time. In fairness to a player who does spend much of his time warming the bench, it must be admitted that being in a good groove—the feeling of over-all correctness that a batter has when his timing is right and his confidence is brim-full (he *knows* he is going to hit the ball solidly)—is very difficult to maintain if he plays only sporadically. Nonetheless, some players do have to sit on the bench, and not a little of the manager's task is to keep them relatively happy and unsulking when they are there.

The Complete Manager

This goes back to the classic managerial responsibility of knowing how to handle men, getting the most out of his material, and other hoary phrases. Probably the most important quality for a manager to have is the ability to act like a manager. He, and he alone, must make decisions. There is always a senior partner, a head chef—in short, a boss. The manager must be the boss of his ball club.

Can one manager actually win ball games that another might lose? The question has been artfully contrived, allowing me to answer that all major-league managers are good, in the sense that they know their baseball, or they wouldn't be in the majors. Also, I think it can be argued that although two managers might differ as to what to do in a given situation, the game that one would lose as a result of his decision would be compensated for by another game he would win because of that decision, while the first manager would be the loser. This rather inverse logic works because baseball is a long season, 162 games long. Over that many games, different approaches to the game tend to even out. Mind you, "different approaches" doesn't mean anything radical, merely legitimate differences in the exercising of one of a specified few options. For example, it is the second inning, the opposition has the bases loaded with none out, and things look grim. However, the pitcher has a history of trouble in the early innings. Once he gets by the first and second innings, he regains his usual good stuff and good control. Do you take him out? If you do, you will be taxing your bullpen, which may be full of arm-weary relievers. Also, you may destroy the pitcher's confidence. A big inning will break the game wide open, turning it into a "laugher"— for your opponents to enjoy.

Perhaps half the time you take the pitcher out. The other times, you may leave him in. Why? Hunch, gamble, guess.* Perhaps. Or perhaps the manager leaves him in because he has a big series coming with the first-place team—or second-place, if his team leads the pack. *This* game is only one game, with a crucial series to follow. Perhaps it is this unrelenting pressure to look ahead which distinguishes the manager in the dugout from the thousands of "managers," in the stands. The fan is involved with the ball game being played *now*. The manager must be concerned with all the ball games that his team plays.

I have always been fascinated by the role of

* The first guess belongs to the manager. The second guess, as we shall no doubt hear more of, belongs to the fan.

the manager. Under the guise of writing this book, I was able to indulge myself. I wrote to the twenty-four major-league managers and asked each the same question: "What is the most difficult decision for a manager to make during the course of the game?" Back came the responses, swiftly from the teams playing at home, straggling in from those on the road. All the managers agreed that the most crucial decision was when to change pitchers. But some of their answers reflected such subtleties of understanding—of the ballplayers, as well as of the game itself—that they are particularly insightful.

Here is what Manager Don Gutteridge of the Chicago White Sox had to say: "Probably the most difficult problem involves the pitcher, whether to leave him in or call in a reliever—and, if so, which one? I may also add another comment. I believe that the biggest problem facing a manager as a manager of men is that of separating personality from ability. Ability is what counts. Ability wins ball games—but managers are human beings, and being human are prone to play a ballplayer with less ability whom they like, in preference to one with more ability whom they don't like. And a manager just can't do that."

Joe Gordon, manager of the Kansas City Royals, agrees that the pitching change is crucial. And he observes: "If the pitcher is good—that is, proven—a manager tends to stay with him longer. Over-all, the manager's day is full of decisions, beginning with his arrival at the ball park. That's when he finds out who is healthy and who isn't, and what problems or developments have occurred overnight which may affect the availability of players in the day's game. This succession of decisions involving personnel culminates with the manager making out his lineup card."

Manager Clyde King of the San Francisco Giants is not about to disagree. "The most difficult decision is *when to remove the pitcher!* And of course this depends on how good your relief pitcher is that you bring in as a replacement. The two things that determine whether or not I take a pitcher out are: 1) if he has lost his stuff, and 2) if he has given up—if he has lost confidence in his ability to win."

Mayo Smith of the Detroit Tigers also concurs. "The crucial decision is, of course, when to change pitchers. In making this decision, the manager must consider the score of the game, the pitcher's physical condition and mental attitude, the effectiveness of the proposed reliever against the existing batting order and possible pinch-hitters, and various other matters. An old-time manager once said of his job, 'There are only two things to managing a ball club—getting along with your players, and knowing when to change pitchers.'"

And here is what St. Louis Cardinal manager Red Schoendienst replied: "Unquestionably, the option to remove a pitcher—or to leave him in the game—is the manager's most difficult decision. It is important not only because it will influence the course of *that* game, but because it may have equal influence upon future games—for example, by changing the pitching rotation, which every manager tries to keep in a predetermined order. Another managerial decision is sort of parallel to changing a pitcher: replacing one ballplayer who is in a slump with another. Both these decisions can powerfully affect the psychology of the ballplayers involved. And psychology, or confidence—or what the players call being in a groove—is all-important in baseball. A ballplayer not only has to be talented. He must *believe*—in himself. Thus, any managerial decision which touches upon the player's cornerstone of self-confidence is extremely important."

Is it true, then, that any manager given "the horses"—the talented ballplayers, that is—will win? Probably. But some managers do seem to get more wins with less-talented players than others. Why?

Why indeed? The question continues to plague us. Probably—and I advance this only hesitantly—the difference is one of human psychology. Some managers are tough, iron-fisted rulers of their clubs. They drive their players and are unloved in return. Others are mild-mannered, soft-spoken men. *Their* players are devoted and drive themselves, presumably. Alas, it doesn't necessarily follow that the hardnosed manager will do any less well than the soft-spoken chap. I say alas because the beloved leader should get more from his players; it's the American way.

Such oversimplifications may be, of themselves, misleading. The truth is that the manager must practice his psychology on an individual basis. One ballplayer may respond only to being chewed out, whether in private or within embarrassing earshot of the crowded bench. Another ballplayer may respond to such public chastisement by sulking, getting even by not doing his job. The manager must know which ballplayer is responsive to what approach.

Leo Durocher, now manager of the Chicago Cubs, has often been quoted as saying, "Nice guys finish last." Allowing for a certain managerial cynicism—it must be the most visible job in the world, with a stadium full of critics ready to tell you when you have gone wrong—I don't think Mr. Durocher meant to be taken literally. Probably what he meant was that the manager has to be the boss.

The Coaches

Nobody knows they're there. Except the players. Yet they are often the most excited figures on the field. They clap their hands and shout encouragement. Occasionally they whisper in the ear of a runner or huddle in foul ground with a batter. They are rarely still—whistling, scratching, moving their arms, tugging at the peaks of their caps, pirouetting gracelessly, or briefly standing flat-footed with arms akimbo. Who are these creatures who cavort so energetically on the field, yet remain largely ignored by those in the stands?

They are coaches.

From their white-ruled rectangles behind third and first base, the coaches help the manager control the game. They do this in two ways. First, by using a secret sign language to convey a specific order from the manager in the dugout to hitter and runner. Second, by making split-second decisions on their own.

Of the two coaches, the busiest and the one with the greatest responsibility is at third base. He is the "sign man," the coach at whom the batter and runner dart glances to see what play, if any, the manager has called for. Signs can tell a batter to take—"do not swing, repeat, *do* *not swing* at the next pitch." A hit sign, not quite conversely, means "You have permission to swing at the next pitch *if* it is a good one to hit." With a runner on first, or runners on first and second, the hit-and-run may be flashed, *requiring* the batter to swing and, it's hoped, make contact.*

1. THE SQUEEZE PLAY

Other signs tell a runner he *may* steal, or *command* two runners on second and first to execute a double steal. Still other signs tell a batter to lay down a sacrifice bunt, or that the squeeze play or safety squeeze is called for.**

---

* Of course, if the count is 3 and 2 the manager may have the runners moving on the pitch and let the batter judge whether he should swing or not, since if the pitch is a ball the batter will walk.

** A squeeze is a surprise play designed to score a runner from third when there is one out or less. The batter feigns his usual stance, implying that he is up at the plate to get a hit. Then he swiftly squares around and bunts. As the pitcher goes into his motion the runner from third suddenly dashes down the line. If the ball is bunted fair, the defense will certainly be unable to get the runner at the plate, and very often the batter will be safe at first with a bunt single. However, should the batter miss the sign and take the pitch, or try to bunt and miss the ball completely, the runner from third will be out by ten feet. Also, the batter may merely tap a soft line drive to an infielder, leaving the runner with the unlikely task of scampering back to third before the fielder can throw him out there. In a variety of ways, the squeeze can be a disaster. Its virtue is overwhelming surprise; when it works, it catches the defense flat-footed.

The safety squeeze is a less perilous version of this play. The runner on third does *not* charge home *until* the batter has laid down his bunt. This requires a somewhat faster runner, since the quotient of surprise

2. THE THIRD-BASE COACH

Most signs are yes-no indicators—to do or not to do a variety of different things: hit, take, run, bunt, and so on. They are transmitted—the inevitable verb is "flashed"—from the manager, who signals to the third-base coach, who passes the sign along to the batter and runner. Most signs are body movements. Almost always they incorporate a key that activates the real sign. All the rest are, naturally, camouflage.

Let's suppose the hit sign is skin-on-skin. The third-base coach rubs his hands together. He claps his hands. He whistles. He rubs his hand on his jaw. He kicks at the dirt. He claps. He takes off his hat. He scratches his head. He moves his hand across the letters on his uniform. He claps his hands. He scratches the small of his back. He stands silent, doing nothing.

The key—the indicator that the next sign was really and truly the one to follow—was the hand brushing the letters of the uniform. Thus the next handclap—skin-on-skin—was the hit sign.

Obviously, if the third-base coach performed his frantic actions only at intervals, the defense would be aware that something was about to happen. This explains the more or less continuous movement that the coach indulges in.

What else does the third-base coach do? He yells at runners on second and third to remind them of how many are out; with two out, of course, the runners should run whenever and wherever the ball is hit—"run on anything" is the rule. With

---

and the runner's start are both lessened. But it entails far less danger to the runner.

fewer than two out, the third-base coach gives the stop or go sign to a runner rounding third.

This is a crucial responsibility. Suppose a ball is lined sharply to the outfield. It is a base hit, yes, but what is the speed of the runner on second? How about the power and accuracy of the out-fielder's arm? The coach has to compute these instantly and tell the runner to hold at third or head on home. And the runner at first—should he stop at second or try for third? Again, the third-base coach has the responsibility. He also tells a runner coming into third whether he can make it standing up or whether he must hit the dirt—slide.

To keep a runner moving, the coach waves his arm in a clockwise motion, an action inevitably accompanied by an excited jumping up and down and a shrill "C'mon, c'mon!" To tell a runner to hold up, or not to slide, the coach raises both hands and extends them imploringly before him. To signal the runner to slide, he leans forward, pushing down on the air before him with both hands. His judgment—to send a runner, to hold a runner—can win a ball game. Or lose it.

Just as coaches wigwag meaninglessly to conceal their meaningful signs, so good players always cast a glance down the third-base line. For if the hitter looks to the coach only in a situation where the defense might logically suspect that a play is on, much of the element of surprise has been lost. However, there are times when a coach will meet the hitter halfway down the line and, with an arm round his shoulder, whisper a play, or nothing, in his ear. Generally, the hitter in this instance is a pitcher, whose lack of expertise at the plate frequently extends to reading signs as well as hitting.*

One other important task of the third-base coach is to make sure that a runner on third base takes his lead in foul ground. This is a form of insurance against the runner's being hit by a batted ball while he and the ball are in fair ground.**

3. THE FIRST-BASE COACH

What does this leave for the first-base coach? Some quite important duties. Remember, there will always be more action at first than at any other base, since more hitters get to first than to the other bases.

The first-base coach is a vocal alarm for the runner. "Move out, move out," he says, encouraging the runner to extend his lead. "Back, back," he implores if he sees the catcher about to try and pick the runner off, or if he sees the second baseman stealthily creeping in behind the runner while the first baseman innocently gazes skyward. On a safe hit to the outfield, the first-base coach may scream, "Two, two," meaning that the batter should try for second. And, like his brother coach

---

* Come on, come on, let's be fair. This happens mostly in situations where the really important thing is that the hitter, pitcher or not, know with absolute certainty what the play is. For example, when the player—often, I admit, a pitcher—is being asked to sacrifice in a situation where that is clearly what he must try to do—i.e., with none out and a runner on first.

** Runners on first or second have no such option, of course. But any runner who is hit by a batted ball in fair territory is out. In such cases the batter is credited with a hit, and the putout goes to the defensive player nearest the unfortunate runner.

across the way, he too constantly reminds the runner of how many are out, and he may caution against taking the extra base because of the outfielder's accurate arm.

If the runner displays some uncertainty as to what sign (if any) is on, the coach will be there, whispering urgent realities in his ear.

When the human telegraph system breaks down, it is usually the player's fault. I don't mean to suggest that hitters or runners are dim-witted or lax. But watching the signs—which means knowing when a play is on and, just as important, when a play has been taken off—demands great concentration from the batter and the runner. And the players fall victim to other demands: concentration in the case of the hitter; enthusiasm in the case of a runner, who may fly through the coach's frantic stop sign at third and be out by the proverbial ten feet at home.

Time was when many managers themselves manned the third-base coaching line. Nowadays this is rare. Contemporary managers apparently prefer the relative peace and solitude of the dugout, where they can scheme in a less exposed position. Or perhaps it is simply that a manager in a coaching box is a sitting duck for the wrath of the fans.

4. THE OTHER COACHES

The coaching staff, by the way, is not limited to the two stalwarts on the lines. There is always at least one other coach, whose specialty is working with pitchers. Not surprisingly, he is called the pitching coach. He is usually a former pitcher of renown or, in more recent years, a catcher. Whatever his background, he toils with the pitchers on the staff, watching for flaws in the motion that affect the delivery, teaching new pitches, and suggesting new ways to heighten the effectiveness of old ones. A fourth coach may be an infield specialist who similarly advises the infielders, and at least one of the coaches will be famous as a hitter. He, of course, counsels on matters of style, stance, and swing.

With all this assistance, you may think there is little for the manager to do. Why, then, do you suppose he worries so much?

Now let's go on to the real boss of the game: the umpire.

The Umpire

The league president shall appoint one or more umpires to officiate at each league championship game. The umpires shall be responsible for the conduct of the game in accordance with these official rules and for maintaining discipline and order on the playing field during the game. . . . Any umpire's decision which involves judgment, such as, but not limited to, whether a batted ball is fair or foul, whether a pitch is a strike or a ball, or whether a runner is safe or out, is final. No player, manager, coach or substitute shall object to any such judgment decisions.—*Official Baseball Rules*

"Steeeriiikkkeee three!" The leather-lunged umpire's call reverberates throughout the stadium. On a called strike three (a pitch which is taken, as opposed to swung at) his authoritative bellow is usually accompanied by a grandiloquent gesture —the right hand briefly held up, then swiftly extended away from the body and jerked back. The voice, the arm movement are unflinching testimony to the umpire's conviction that he is absolutely and unequivocally right.

To which the fan whose baseball education is already well along will say, "Oh, yeah?"

And to which I reply, "Yeah."

The active officials—those whose duties call for them to rule while the game is in progress—are crucial to the outcome of any sport. But the degree of leverage that official judgment exerts varies from sport to sport. Thus, the service linesman's call of "fault" in a tennis match is on a relatively low level of influence. Over the full course of game, set, match, that call may prove important, but only very rarely will it be vital. A decision of a football or basketball official can powerfully affect the outcome of the game, but such a judgment is rendered within the context of massive and confused action. In effect, the accuracy or inaccuracy of the ruling is masked by a jumble of active players.

Not so the baseball umpire. His decisions—any one of which may prove crucial—are made in the open, in full view of everyone in the stadium: players, managers, fans. And not always are those decisions popular, or even grudgingly agreed with.

One result of the umpire's regulatory nakedness is that on any close call some of the participants and spectators are sure to disagree, volubly and even violently. In the face of the constant threat (and frequent appearance) of such disagreement, umpires often seek refuge in their tyrannical power. The heady feeling of total authority is based on fact, for, quite literally, every technical point of the game must be decided by umpirical wisdom: fair ball or foul; ball or strike; out or safe; appeal play allowed or disallowed; a ball touched by a fan and therefore subject to predetermined ground rules, or still in play; legal pitching motion or illegal balk; the weather permits or does not permit the game to continue—and more.

It is hardly surprising that, as the story goes, when a player impatiently asked the umpire, "What was it, safe or out?" the umpire replied, "It ain't nothing until I call it."

The personality of an umpire is important just because of the disputatious nature of his calling. Bench jockeys from both dugouts sharpen their needles for him.* Because their majestic authority is their protection, umpires are particularly susceptible to the bench jockey's barbs. When the back of the umpire's neck progresses from pink to deep purple, the offending player will be warned. Literally: "One more word, Gibson, and you're outa the game." One word and he is, too.**

---

* A bench jockey is a player who is riding the bench and tends to spur the tender epidermis of the umpire with taunts. Bench jockeys are sometimes vicious, sometimes reasonably good-humored. Vicious or not, the jocks don't pick only on umpires. Sometimes a team is enraged by something an opposing ballplayer has done. When that happens they may ride the offending player unmercifully—not only in that one game or throughout a series of games, but all season long.

** Umpires try to ignore bench jockeys, following the old principle that the best way to discourage such attention-getting devices is to ignore them. However, if the dugout commentary is excessive—a very personal judgment made individually by each umpire— the umpire will eject the ball player he *thinks* is responsible for the unflattering comments. The evicted dugout tenant is often an innocent bysitter, while the real culprit chortles with his hand over his mouth. However, if the innocent but banished player is a regular, or one whose absent services eventually cause the game to be lost, the manager will exact some appropriate tribute from the true malefactor. Thus justice has triumphed, more or less. I must point out that my

Personality is an important element in umpiring because the volatile arbiter is likely to blow not only his cool but his call. The basic characteristic of good umpiring—and, I suppose, of officiating in any sport—is consistency. This is particularly true of calling balls and strikes. The strike zone, you may recall, is that space over home plate which is between the batter's armpits and the tops of his knees when he assumes his natural stance. My estimate of knee-tops and yours might vary. Also, the hitter's "natural stance" can distort even the boniest knees and muscle-ridged armpits, further enlarging the scope of personal umpirical judgment. But as long as an umpire is consistent in his interpretation of the official rule, order will prevail.

The Plate Umpire

Interestingly enough, National League plate umpires work from a skewed position between the catcher and the batter, which gives the umpire a perspective that is somewhat off-center. American League umpires position themselves immediately behind the catcher, looking over and past his shoulder and head. This may account for the belief widely held by players, managers, and sportswriters that National League umpires "give" the pitcher a low strike, while their American League brothers bestow a high strike.*

---

wife's personalization of the player threatened with ejection from the game is highly irrelevant. I am mild, meek, and soft-spoken—and anyway, pitchers can't afford to antagonize umpires.

* I don't know of a single ballplayer who has ever pitched or batted in a game arbitered by an umpire from the other league (the one other than that in

As a normal matter, a crew of four umpires works a major-league game. The umpire-in-chief for the day is always the plate umpire—a responsibility which is rotated among the umpires on a single-game basis. Another umpire is at first base, one is at second, the fourth is behind third base.

The plate umpire is responsible for the generalized proper conduct of the game. His duties are: to call balls and strikes; to declare fair and foul balls, except when the other umps, the field umpires, have geographical jurisdiction; to make all decisions except those commonly reserved for the field umpires; to inform the official scorer of the official batting order and any subsequent changes; to announce any special ground rules; to announce a time limit for a game (if one has been set) before the game starts; to decide when a game shall be forfeited.*

---

which he normally plays) who will disagree with this assertion. As a practical matter, the difference is this: in the National League an umpire is disposed to call a borderline high pitch above the letters a ball. In the American League the situation is reversed, with questionable high pitches getting the strike call, while debatable low pitches tend to be balls. This difference may help explain why a batter who has always had trouble with low pitches in the National League will be a much improved hitter in the American; the pitches he formerly took that were strikes are now balls. As it happens, I am a high-ball pitcher, and I am convinced that if I pitched in the American League I would probably issue fewer walks.

* Games aren't forfeited very often. The last time was in July of 1954. The Cardinals were playing the Philadelphia Phillies in a Sunday doubleheader. It was, history tells us, a blistering hot day. The Cards lost the first game 11–10. In the second, the Cards were behind 8–1 in the fifth inning. The fire-eating Cardinal manager, Eddie (the Brat) Stanky, capped a series of

Until a ball game starts, the home team has the option of deciding whether or not the game can get under way; it may be raining, or the field may be too wet to play on. Once it is officially under way—once the batting lineups are handed to the plate umpire—the game is in the hands of the umpires.

It is fascinating to explore what would happen in a game if the unthinkable happened, the impossible occurred. Umpires, of course, play a prominent role in such speculation. But very broadly, the most important decisions by umpires are those of balls and strikes (exclusively the province of the plate umpire, of course), safe or out (on the bases, including home), and position of the ball (whether fair or foul, in the stands or out, caught or trapped).

The Base Umpires
The first-base umpire has most of the safe or out calls, many of them of the look-and-listen variety described in the section on "The Field." In case of a tie—the fielder's throw and the batter-runner arriving at first base simultaneously—the runner is declared safe.

The umpire at second base is most frequently

---

fights, arguments, and assorted delaying tactics by signaling with vague indirection for a new pitcher. "Who," said the plate umpire, "are you bringing in?" "Corcoran," said Stanky. "Who?" said the umpire, recalling that no pitcher—indeed, no player—of that name appeared on the Cardinal roster. "Corcoran," said Stanky. "He's a pitcher in Rochester. He oughta be able to catch the next train." That did it. The game was declared forfeited to Philadelphia by the score of 9–0—the prescribed score of all forfeited games.

confronted with double plays and steals. For the former, his major concern will be whether the pivot man—the member of the DP combination who is fed the ball and who must pivot and throw to first—has possession of the ball when his foot touches the bag. Possession means firm, unjuggled control of the ball. And the pivot man's foot must touch the bag neither before nor after he has possession, but while he does. There is a certain amount of allowance made for the heavy traffic around second during the double play— that is, the attempt of the runner from first to slide into, perhaps bowling over and possibly injuring, the pivot man. I am not suggesting that umpires allow the pivot man to fake his job, but on the other hand the umpire isn't there to enforce the rule so literally that injury to one or both players is inevitable.

On a steal, the umpire must watch two things: when the runner actually reaches the base, and when the tag is made. The tag may be tardy or errant, or the runner's feet may go over the bag, yet not touch the bag until after the tag is made.

On these plays the umpire is generally right. He is on top of the play, and the fan is not, while players on the bench, because of the turtle-back nature of the infield and the "sunken" construction of the dugout, may be able to see only the upper portions of the bodies of those involved. The first- and third-base umpires rule on whether a ball is fair or foul down the right- and left-field lines respectively. All three field umpires will also charge out into the outfield to be as close as possible to the point where the catch is made and rule on whether a legal catch was made or the ball was trapped. This is a somewhat more difficult call, for oftentimes when an outfielder appears to have picked a ball off his shoetops he has trapped it—smothered it between glove and grass so smoothly and swiftly that it appears to have been caught.

The field umpires do a considerable amount of shifting, to one side of a base or another, back a bit, in a trifle, and so on. This is because umpires try to anticipate where a play is likely to occur and assume a position enabling them to get the best perspective on the expected play.

Probably the most difficult umpiring call is that of the plate umpire when the batter takes a half-swing. Did he "break his wrists," in which case the pitch is a strike, for the batter has, by umpirical definition, swung? If he didn't break his wrists, the pitch is a ball, for obviously if it was a called strike it would make no difference what the batter did. In such instances, the plate umpire may direct a questioning look at the first- or third-base umpire. If the response is a nod, the consulted field ump is saying, "Yes, he did swing." A shake of the head means, "No, he didn't swing." This is one of the few frequently observable instances in which one umpire seeks assistance from another. And, as I have suggested, even this consultation is far from obvious.

The Umpire's Life

The line between the umpire's blue-suited majesty and his human fallibility is thin. But don't forget that the umpire is constantly threatened with vociferous disagreements. There are managers, for example, who seem to believe that not arguing with an umpire—even when the umpire is right, or at least the manager, from his poor viewing position in the dugout, cannot possibly have observed anything about which to disagree—will be interpreted by their players as a sign of weakness. I doubt that this is so. But surely the frequency of baseless arguments feeds the fires of an umpire's self-righteousness and discourages him from ever, in any way, admitting that he has missed the play—by seeking the opinion of another umpire, for example. Of course no umpire will ever overrule another, unless the whole business is cloaked with the reasonableness of consulting. And that, as previously indicated, doesn't happen too often.*

The umpire's life isn't easy. As we have seen, he works under great pressure and is subject to abuse and vilification. And through it all he is required to remain aloof from vindictiveness, from the desire to punish a player or manager *today* for something he said *yesterday.* Nor may he compensate for a self-admitted bad decision against one player by giving him the benefit of the doubt on a close call later on.

Umpires may be the most theatrical figures on the field. The already-described exuberance of

* I recall once trying to score from third on an infield grounder. The throw to the catcher was high, and everyone in the ball park knew I was safe. "Out," the umpire, who shall remain nameless, declared. The catcher walked away, too embarrassed to stay at the plate and witness the legitimate beef he expected. At this point the umpire leaned over and whispered, in an agony of contrition, "Bob, I missed the play." Of course, there was nothing I could say in the face of such surprising candor, nor could the plate umpire seek another opinion. The play was his to call. Although you may interpret this little story as being critical, I should prefer that you believe that it left me, finally, with a sense of respect for the man's honesty. Umpires are human—I guess.

called strike three is but one dramatic gesture. There are others. The out sign at any base but first usually is the result of some less-than-common action: attempted steal; a single that could not be stretched into a double; a runner taking the extra base or trying to score. On such plays the umpires seem to respond unconsciously to the heightened drama of the moment. The call is made loudly, and the right arm is cocked low in front, then swept high and around with the thumb standing straight out in the definitive sign: "Yer out." However, the umpire is equally ready to gratify the hometown crowd with a barked declaration of "Safe"—the happy news being accompanied by the arms held behind and away from the body, palms down, in something resembling a caricature of a swimmer poised for a racing dive.

In addition to his somewhat strenuous calisthenics, the plate umpire keeps his fingers nimble by keeping the ball-and-strike count on a plastic counter especially suited to this purpose.

All umpires must know the rule book backward and forward, not only literally, in terms of explicit rulings as they relate to certain game situations, but also as regards the interpretation of the rules when they must apply—by extension, as it were—to some rather strange situations.

For example, there's a runner on first and none out. The pitcher is at bat and, as expected, lays down a sacrifice bunt, and sprints down toward first, straddling the line. The catcher pounces on the ball and throws to first, but the throw hits the pitcher in the back and rolls away. What should the ump do?

Ruling: Because the batter-runner straddled the line—that is, he was not solely in the special

three-foot lane provided expressly for his use—
he is guilty of interference and is out. The ball
is declared dead, and the runner who was on
first must remain there. (Sharp-eyed, long-mem-
oried readers will recall that way back in "The
Field" I promised to return to the subject of the
three-foot lane.)

Or tackle this one. The batter hits a high fly
ball to right field. The right fielder ambles in
a couple of steps and camps beneath it. Suddenly
the startled outfielder sees a pigeon fly directly
into the ball. Recovering quickly, the right fielder
catches the ball before it hits the ground, while the
hungry center fielder snares the bird. What is the
appropriate ruling?

The batter can't be out because the ball is not
legally "in flight," so that any catch is unlawful.
The ball remains in play, with the runner entitled
to get as many bases as he can, at his own risk.
The pigeon? The center fielder is allowed to keep
it, unless he wants to give the umpire the bird.

Hesitantly, I offer this final head-scratcher. The
bases are loaded, two men are out, and a tough
hitter is at the plate. With the count 3 and 2,
the batter hits a high foul fly near third base.
The wind catches the ball and pushes it closer and
closer to the stands. The third baseman is in hot
pursuit and finally comes smack up against the
box-seats railing. With a desperate lunge he reaches
as far into the stands as he can, but just as he
seems to have speared the ball a fan knocks it
out of his glove. How would you rule? And never
mind about the fan; he is hero or heretic, according to whether he helps or hurts the team you
root for. As to his sense of sportsmanship—well,
the less said of that the better.

Ruling: A fielder who reaches into the stands to make a catch does so at his own risk. Thus there is no call of interference or anything else. The foul ball is simply a foul ball.

I have selected these examples only to suggest some of the varied questions on which an umpire must be prepared to issue a firmly voiced, soundly reasoned decision. There are relatively few fans who are more than generally conversant with the rules of baseball, and even these are more concerned with the results of a ruling than with the rule itself. It is not necessary that you arm yourself with the precedent-seeking mind of an umpire. As your experience as a baseball fan increases, you will absorb enough of the logic of the game to enable you to disagree with the umpire on your own terms.

The maturing fan will almost surely desire to express herself about some of the finer points of the game, and not a few of these will be found in the following chapter.

The Finer Points

An Infield Fly is a fair fly ball (not including a line drive nor an attempted bunt) which can be caught by an infielder with ordinary effort, when first and second, or first, second and third bases are occupied, before two are out. The pitcher, catcher and any outfielder who stations himself in the infield on the play shall be considered infielders for the purpose of this rule. When it seems apparent that a batted ball will be an Infield Fly, the umpire shall immediately declare "Infield Fly" for the benefit of the runners. If the ball is near the baselines, the umpire shall declare "Infield Fly, if Fair." The ball is alive and runners may advance at the risk of the ball being caught, or retouch and advance after the ball is touched, the same as on any fly ball. If the hit becomes a foul ball it is treated the same as any foul ball.—*Official Baseball Rules*

The Infield Fly

When the infield-fly ruling is invoked, the batter is automatically out. Notice that the ruling applies only when there are runners aboard, first base is occupied, and there are fewer than two out. The purpose of this ruling is to protect the team at bat. How can that be, if the batter is declared automatically out?

Well, in days of unscrupulous yore, canny infielders would intentionally drop an infield fly, and the runners, without the assurance that they could not be forced, were caught between the option to run—in which case the fielder *would* catch the ball on the fly and easily double up the runner—or not to run, in which case the fielder would not catch the ball and would still have an easy double play. Thus, although the infield-fly rule automatically erases the batter, it protects the scoring threat posed by the runners.*

Note that the infield-fly rule applies only to a fair ball. If it's foul, the ball must be caught, for otherwise the batter is not out and it is merely a foul strike if there are fewer than two strikes on the batter.

Although the infield-fly rule may be puzzling at first, its logic will become clear on reflection. Certainly no one can miss its application, for the umpire will declare himself loudly, the coaches will echo him, the batter will throw his bat away in obvious disgust, and radio and television announcers will weightily note that the infield-fly ruling has been invoked.

There are many aspects of baseball which superficially appear simple, yet are based on hours and hours of practice culminating in the easy mastery the average fan takes for granted. And lord knows no woman wants to be considered average! More-

* Once the umpire has declared, "Infield fly," the batter is out even if the infielders do not catch the ball. However, they usually do, since a baseball striking a sun-baked infield or a pebble has been known to carom wildly away, in which case the runners, free to advance at their own risk, will certainly do so. By the way, when the quotation from the official rules says "retouch," it means the same as the more familiar "tag up."

over, and most deliciously, the points that follow will probably give you the opportunity to off-handedly drop some quite professional comments into the conversation when your husband, eager to display his knowledge, discovers that you are reading a book about baseball.

Base-Running

For example, let us consider the fine art of base-running. Actually, base-running begins at home (there is a possibly funny witticism to be made of this, but I'll let it pass), and not only in the most obvious sense that the batter must get a hit or a walk, or—less frequently, of course—reach base as a result of a fielding error. The batter has to practice getting away from the plate as quickly as possible. An instant's delay can result in an out rather than a hit, or a single rather than a double. Therefore, a batter practices not only hitting but the technique of regaining his balance after the pattern of bat-swing and follow-through has been completed. With one or two strides he is out of the box and winging toward first. He will try to hit the middle of the (first-base) bag with his toe, the leg extended at full stride. This *doesn't* mean that he will do a couple of dance steps to make sure that his foot is fully extended. Through practice, he has learned to get down the line at maximum speed and with a rhythm to his running that will enable him to hit the bag more or less as I have indicated. Any feet-shuffling along the way simply slows the batter and helps the infielders.

But if the batter has hit a ground ball that has gone through the infield, or a line drive to the outfield, as he approaches first base the coach will yell at him to "take your turn." This means the hitter-runner will swerve to the right before reaching the bag, then cut back to the left so that he touches the inside corner of the bag. This enables him to touch first and accomplish the narrowest possible turn, with the result that he can stick to the "inside of the track"; he is now heading toward, or at least facing, second base.

Taking a turn means that the coach has given assurance that the batter has a single—but the outfielders may misplay the ball. The turn puts the batter-runner in position to capitalize on any defensive mistakes. You may sometimes hear that a hitter takes a "very wide turn at first," which simply means that, instead of proceeding past first base a very few steps, he has progressed, somewhat daringly, a bit farther toward second. You may hear an announcer say that "he rounds first and now holds there," which means the same thing. But when you hear that a hitter "rounds first and heads for second" we have a different situation. On advice of counsel (the coach), the batter is trying for a double. If there is no chance that the throw will arrive at the base in time to endanger the runner, he will go in standing up—without sliding. But frequently he will have to hit the dirt.

Sliding
Sliding is falling by design, always under control. The runner merely drops to the ground, and his momentum does the rest. It isn't quite as easy as it sounds but, paradoxically, although it looks rather difficult, it is far less so than many other elements of the game.

A good slide begins with good timing. If the runner slides too early his momentum will vanish and he'll wind up sprawled in the basepath several feet short of the bag. If he is too late, his momentum will carry him past the bag. Most players slide with their heads back, arms raised, fingers clenched loosely to avoid injury. There are several different ways of sliding, the most common being the bent-leg slide. In this version the right leg is tucked under the left leg at a maximum angle. The slider slides on the calf of the bent leg. The left leg is kept firm but loose, with the heel off the ground, and of course it is the left leg which touches the bag. A variation of this slide, probably accounting for its popularity, enables the runner to slide smoothly into the bag and just as smoothly pop up onto two feet again. This is accomplished mostly through putting his left hand down, palm to the ground, and levering off of the slide into an upright position.

All slides have a strong flavor of excitement, which no doubt stems from the accompanying cloud of dust, though the hearty "Hi-ho, Silver" is absent. By far the most dramatic slide is head-first, which can best be explained by saying that it is a bellyflop on *terra firma*, combined with elements of kamikaze and desire. Actually, it's not that bad, but the risk of injury is somewhat greater than in the other variations.*

* A batter trying for first will sometimes use a head-first slide if, because of where the ball was hit, the first baseman or covering fielder has to make a swipe tag at him rather than try to get to the bag. The head-first slide is also used in moments of maximum peril— getting back to first when the pitcher is trying to pick the runner off, for example. One other sliding variation is the hook slide, in which the runner allows his

The Weather

Perhaps the finest point of all has to do with weather and the score. To be recognized as "legal," a baseball game must go four and one-half innings *if* the home team is ahead, or five *full* innings if the home team is tied or behind. The major cause of suspended play, and then, perhaps, of the game's being washed away, is the weather.

Once the umpire suspends play because of the weather, he must wait a mandatory thirty minutes before declaring the game either postponed—in which case, if the necessary number of innings were not played, all the hits, errors, and other details are as if they never happened—or suspended, which means that the necessary innings have been completed, the score stands according to the operative rules, and the game is, though abbreviated, official and takes its place in the record book.

Now a manager whose team is losing and who perceives that the sky is filled with dark clouds will, when the crucial fourth inning approaches, attempt to delay matters in any way he can. On order, his batters will step into and out of the box, return to the dugout for different bats, find

---

momentum to carry him past the bag but "hooks" the bag with his foot. Almost all slides are evasive, designed to elude a tag—except the body-block slide, which a runner uses to try and break up a double play. In such instances, the idea is to roll your body into the second baseman and, football-fashion, flatten him. When this is accomplished, the fielder and base-runner have been known to throw a few punches. A similar but slightly less aggressive tactic is to slide more or less normally, but try to hook the pivot man's foot with your own, causing him, to put it delicately, to lose his balance.

dust in their eyes which must be removed by the trainer (impatiently summoned onto the field by the umpire), and in other ways make all the usual actions take as much time as possible. If his team is in the field, he may change pitchers, but only after prolonged consultation with the catcher and his present pitcher. And having brought in one new pitcher—who must pitch to one batter until that batter is either retired or reaches base—he may change pitchers again. Even the golf carts on which pitchers now ride in from the bullpen have been known, under certain climatic conditions or threat of same, to break down. All the while one manager is praying for rain, and more or less artfully contriving to make the progress of the game wait for it, the other manager is screaming at the umpire about manager number one's deceitful and unsportsmanlike practice, pleading to get on with the game.

Certainly I would not wish to be accused of delaying the game, particularly when your seat is ready.

The Game

"Charley, be sure and get there early so I can see you when I'm warming up, just as you did when I won last week."—Robert Gibson's Rules for Rooting Wives, or, Don't Change Anything if You're Winning

It is spring. Not the sometimes false spring of March 21, a chilly, damp mockery of the calendar's declaration, but truly spring. The sun is no longer simply a shining orb of cold light. The air is warm, the breeze is gentle, the trees have covered their winter's nakedness, and from Seattle to Boston, Atlanta to Montreal, the country stirs with the promise of change—from cold to warm in some areas, from warm to hot in others.

The ball parks, too, have marked the season. The empty seats have been freshly painted but still stare sightlessly down on the quiet playing field. The field itself has surely been sodded with lush green grass (or Astroturf), against which the whiteness of the foul lines gleams with hospital-like severity; the skin part of the infield is a rich brown in contrast.

Getting Ready
We are very early. The game will not start for some hours. But although the field is still deserted,

124

there is life in many chambers and corners within the complexities of the stadium's fortress-like walls. In storerooms and kitchens thousands of hot dogs are being readied for their fate and a regiment of mustard jars are being filled. Venders' equipment—back-packed dispensers for coffee, portable racks for beer, over-the-shoulder insulated containers for ice cream—lies clean and polished, waiting to be shouldered by teen-agers or mature men, each of whom will pause during a crucial part of the game to watch the action, oblivious of the impatient calls from hungry and thirsty fans. Elsewhere pennants and souvenir pins, the day's programs and the home team's yearbooks lie in cartons, waiting to be waved or worn, annotated by fans who keep their own score or read with delight later on.

In his office, the general manager casts an appraising eye out his window, warily alert for the appearance of clouds that may threaten rain and a smaller crowd, or even postponement of the game. The head groundskeeper looks out at the field and silently prays that the outfielders will not tear up too many divots. An organist puts down a sheaf of music and idly drums her fingers across the wood of the shuttered keyboard. Behind the scoreboard, a technician surveys the controls that enable him to report to the fans not only what the half-inning progress is at this stadium, but also what other teams are doing, as well as projecting onto an enormous message board the words to the National Anthem, baseball brain-teasers, and animated drawings or cheer-inspiring slogans. Elsewhere, the public-address announcer gargles noisily, the umpires dress quietly, and players don their uniforms with whatever attitude the approaching game inspires —quiet desperation from the rookies, wisecracking expectancy by the veterans, and the perpetual optimism of the manager.

Batting Practice

It is now some three hours before the game, and there is the first sign of stirring in the two dugouts. Equipment managers bring out armloads of bats and stack them in the racks at the ends of the dugouts. In a few minutes the home team pours out onto the field, resplendent in pinstripes or bright colors. The appearance is greeted with a ragged cheer and a mild explosion of clapping. We look around and notice that the stands are no longer empty. As in a giant crossword puzzle whose blank spaces are slowly filled in, more and more seats are being occupied. Some of the players head for the batting cage, a large wire-netted square, open on one end, which has been trundled up to the plate, and take their practice cuts— swings—at the deliveries of the batting-practice pitcher. In a strange reversal of the game, he is not trying to get the batter out. Instead, he throws the kind of pitch the hitter requests— curves if the hitter has been having trouble with curves, sliders if these have been a problem. The batting-practice pitcher may be the pitching coach, a relief pitcher who is not expected to see action that day, or a former major-leaguer who now performs only this special task. Because he is feeding the hitters what they want, he deserves special protection. He gets it from a portable screen set up in front of the pitching mound as at least a partial shield against line drives.

After a time, the home team melts away as the

players straggle back to their dugout. Now the subdued uniforms of the visiting team flow onto the field for batting practice.

Infield Practice

The players' defensive skills are not neglected. There will be infield practice, with a coach hitting grounders in rotation to each of the fielders and occasionally directing, "Get two," meaning that the double play should be practiced against invisible runners. And down one of the foul lines a coach is hitting "fungoes," high fly balls which he swats effortlessly with an easy virtuosity that is the envy of small boys everywhere. With his left hand he tosses a baseball into the air, then swiftly gets both hands on the handle of the bat, and expertly times his swing to connect with the vertically dropping ball.*

And the stadium continues to fill with people. Now there is organ music over the public-address system, contributing to the festive atmosphere, an overlay of confidence which hides the question mark posed by the game itself.

Only a few minutes before game time, the last players leave the field. One by one they are swallowed up by the dugout and pass into the clubhouse beyond. Several players respond to the pleading cries of small boys who have clustered in the aisles next to the field boxes. Each boy is almost certainly wearing a miniature of the official team cap the players wear. Absolutely certainly, each boy is armed with a pencil and a program, or perhaps he has brought along his

* Appropriately, fungoes are hit with a fungo bat, which is lighter and longer than that allowed for the actual game.

own baseball to be autographed, or a book containing the treasured signatures of his other sports heroes. In no time what was a handful of youngsters swells to a noisy crowd, all crying impatiently, "Please, Joe, please, Rocky, please, please . . ." For a time the ballplayers scribble furiously and then, as though frightened by the clamor around them, they apologetically back away, escaping to the safety of the clubhouse. Meanwhile the starting pitchers have begun to warm up.

The ground crew trails its rakes and brushes as it smooths the earth that has been torn during practice, and some of its members stamp the white outlines of the batter's and catcher's boxes.

There is an electronic squawk and crackle as the public-address system comes to multi-decibel life. "Good afternoon, ladies and gentlemen. Here is the batting order. For the visiting [whomever], leading off and playing short, Tom Smith." The voice continues with notable impartiality, listing the batting order amid a chorus of boos—with the exception of the mention of a great star, whose career merits a ripple of applause, reflecting the respect of fans that transcends the fanatical loyalty they give to their own team.

Now both dugouts are reoccupied, the players stirring around but not yet taking the field. There is a small cluster of uniforms around home plate, and the keen-eyed observer will note that when a hand absently pushes a baseball cap aside a naked pate reflects the sunlight. The two managers are meeting with the umpires to discuss ground rules and exchange lineup cards.*

---

* Each manager gives one lineup card to the plate umpire and another to the opposing manager. In-

The home team erupts from the dugout, the players running briskly to their positions. The organist salutes their entrance by playing the team song, or, failing that, an organ equivalent of the cavalry bugler's charge or a song in which the home team's city is prominently mentioned. Cheers and handclapping flower in every corner of the stands, but there is an odd, rather perfunctory note to the applause and encouragement. For the game has still not started, and the peculiar emotional chemistry that only baseball can stimulate has not yet begun to affect the fans. They have not lost themselves in the game, not agonized over missed scoring opportunities or bad breaks, exulted in a beautiful defensive play or a timely hit. Not yet.

The public-address system, which has been briefly silent, now hums into life again. "Ladies and gentlemen, our National Anthem." Hats held across their hearts, the players stand facing the flag flying from its mast in center field. The fans come to their feet and listen to the organist playing, and sometimes sing "The Star-Spangled Banner" quietly to themselves. The anthem and singing end, and there are more scattered cheers.

A few moments pass, during which the outfielders play catch among themselves, the infielders practice picking up ground balls thrown to them by the first baseman, each man fielding the easy grounder with exaggerated nonchalance in a kind of unknowing caricature of himself. The pitcher is taking his final warmup tosses, throwing now from the mound with the same in-

---

terestingly, if there is a difference between the two, it is the one handed to the umpire that is official.

tensity and conviction he will exhibit during the game itself.

Off to one side of the plate the leadoff hitter is swinging a couple of bats, the epitome of self-confidence and controlled power. The catcher throws the ball down to second, both as a practice toss and as a ritual. The second baseman spears it with his glove just above the bag, then flips to the shortstop, who fires the ball to the first base-man, who sidearms it across to the third baseman, who very, very easily tosses it to the pitcher.

Play Ball!

The umpire turns his head and says something inaudible from where we are sitting—but surely it must be "Play ball!"—and waves the hitter into the box.

The game has begun. And now . . .

And now comes all agony and delight. The desperate anxiety of victory which may slip from your grasp, or of a rally which may carry you to victory. Now comes the sweetness of your pitcher blazing a high hard one past the vainly swinging batter who goes down with the bases loaded and you're out of the inning; of your left fielder, his cocked bat vibrating as though under enormous tension and then suddenly released to whip around and send the blurred whiteness of the ball riding out and far and over the wall— and you knew it when you heard the meaty hard sound of the fat part of the bat solidly connecting with the ball and you rise to your feet screaming with excitement, even if you're not sure why. And now it is the ground-eating graceful lope of a fielder who unhurriedly arrives at precisely the right moment to catch a fly ball, or his panicked race in pursuit of a line drive that is curving away from him, his cap driven from his head as he dives through the air to make the impossible catch an improbable reality.

Baseball is all these things, and moods and moments of excitement, of delight and sorrowful defeat, of men whose shoulders sag as they walk off the field and who cannot see the dugout because their eyes are filled with tears, and also of handshaking, rump-patting congratulations during which the entire dugout seems to smile.

And why, you ask, have I spent so much time describing what leads up to the game and, in a chapter deceptively called "The Game," why do I now pause without describing a game, a real game?

I cannot. The ebb and flow of tension, the expectancy of the unexpected that accompanies every pitch, every play, is not reducible to an inning-by-inning recapitulation. This is something you feel rather than know—a discreet awareness that marks the fan, who is the subject of our next chapter.

The Fan

"Ya bum, ya couldn't find the plate with a road map."

"Hey, Stone Fingers, my mother can field better than that."

"C'mon, c'mon—oh, beUtiful."

"A ball? He called it a ball? He's deaf, dumb, *and* blind."

"What an arm. Beautiful."

"Just a single. Please, a single's all we need."

"Did y'see that? Why doesn't he open his eyes when he swings?"

"I love ya, ya bum."

—From Charline Gibson's notes from the stands

The fan is more a state of mind than a physical presence. There are servicemen stationed overseas who haven't seen a ball game in several years but who follow their favorite teams as avidly as if they were around the corner. There are blind people who love baseball and regularly listen to the games on radio. (I remember listening to a telephone-talk sports program on a visit to New York, when a blind Mets fan called to discuss a fairly esoteric baseball point. In the ensuing conversation he revealed that his wife, who was not blind, transcribed box scores into braille for him, and that both of them frequently attended games at Shea Stadium.) In a small town practically the entire population will follow the career of one of the local boys who is playing professional ball, noting his progress from the most minor of the minor leagues up to glory, or into obscurity. Fans are knowledgeable and loyal, ignorant and fickle. Fans are cruel and compassionate. Fans can help or hurt a team. Fans are idiosyncratic and yet often herdlike in their behavior. And though all fans share an excited interest in baseball, the fans in St. Louis are markedly different from those in Philadelphia, and New York fans are not the same as those in Los Angeles. The fan is you, and you are an individual, not an interchangeable spectator representative of people living a thousand miles away.

The Brooklyn Fan

I guess that the prototype of the fan is buried under the hallowed ground of Ebbets Field in Brooklyn on a site now occupied by an apartment house. Although the Brooklyn Dodgers have long since become the Los Angeles Dodgers, there still clings to the Dodgers a tradition of irreverent loyalty that has become a cliché, one inseparable from the image of baseball fans everywhere.

Ebbets Field was a very small ball park. It was not a particularly good place to watch a ball game, in the sense that many of the seats provided acute angles of observation, or views that were partially obstructed. But the smallness of the park generated a remarkable sense of intimacy. Moreover, for reasons that elude me (no doubt because I was born in Omaha, Nebraska), the mere mention of Brooklyn provokes a smile or a cheer. For example, if a contestant on a television quiz show says he's from Brooklyn, the MC merely has to look out at the audience to kindle instantaneous laughter and applause. At any rate, this kind of municipal fun-poking, no matter how good-humored, probably helped to polarize the support for the team. Then too, for a number of years the Dodgers were improbable heroes. Even during the years before they became a powerhouse—during the last decade of their tenure in Ebbets Field—the Dodgers had some fine ballplayers. But they were better known for such incidents as having three runners on third base simultaneously, or an outfielder who was hit on the head by a fly ball he was vainly trying to catch.

The Dodger fan's loyalty to his team was hardened through years of frustration. Because of the small size of the ball park, the fans shared a physical as well as spiritual intimacy that also enveloped the ballplayers, who were within easy screaming distance of the stands. Another factor in the syndrome that bound Brooklyn player and fan together was the team's rivalry with the hated New York Giants (pronounced, I am told, "Jints") who dwelt in the Polo Grounds in Manhattan. Like Brooklyn, Manhattan is a borough of the City of New York, but whereas the name Brooklyn had overtones of being—uh—*déclassé*, Manhattan was, and is, a word that connotes luxury, power, and a kind of super-city arrogance.*

* At this point in history there were three major-league teams in New York: the Brooklyn Dodgers; the New York Giants, in Manhattan; and the New York Yankees, in the Bronx, another borough of the city. The Yankees not only had a borough to themselves but were in a class by themselves.

For reasons both sociological and psychological, the Brooklyn Dodger fan was passionately loyal, irreverent, rude, critical, and highly knowledgeable about the game. He could call a favorite player a bum and make the epithet a term of endearment, and he could apply the same word to the Enemy and fill it with medieval loathing. (One of the most famous Dodger fans was Hilda (Cowbells) Chester, a cheerleader *extraordinaire*. So you see, a woman *can* become a baseball legend as well as a fan.)

Everything I have read about the Brooklyn Dodgers and their fans suggests that going to a baseball game at Ebbets Field was fun. This is meaningful on the most basic level, for every team must lose some games, and there can be only two teams which can win a pennant and only one that can win a World Series. The rest of the teams, and their legions of fans, will be disappointed—at least so far as this year is concerned. Here another of the cries of old-time Dodger fans should be recalled to contemporary audiences: "Wait till next year." Except for the supporters of the team that wins, baseball fans live on great expectations—a situation that is certainly a reflection of life beyond the ball-park walls.

Although no baseball fan thinks of himself, or herself, as merely occupying a seat in a stadium, many fans do not realize that they can and do exert considerable influence on the performance of the players. This is accomplished in two ways.

The Players' Reactions to the Fan
First, a team, a player, can *feel* when a crowd

is pulling for it, for him. Your individual cheers may not be literally identifiable, but a chorus of up to fifty or sixty *thousand* people has the ability to get adrenalin flowing in a way that not even a manager's exhortations can. It is easy to over-dramatize this, to write glowingly of the faith in himself that a player can discover or rediscover when he knows that the fans are with him. That may be overdramatic; it is also frequently true.

Second, it is equally true that the opposite crowd reaction can have an effect. I remember a couple of years ago when Robert was the starting pitcher and was shelled for seven runs in the first inning. Finally he was removed for a relief pitcher and started off the mound, trudging slowly toward the dugout, disconsolation visible in his sagging shoulders and dejection written on his face. The polite applause of the fans suddenly changed to a swelling chorus of boos. For a minute he paused and looked up at the stands in disbelief. He had been a fine pitcher for the Cardinals for several years, and in that instant he felt both bewildered and betrayed by the fans' reaction.*

* That's overstating the case a bit. A ballplayer wraps his feelings in professional cynicism, or tries to. He usually says that the fans have paid their money and are entitled to boo or cheer, according to which-ever spirit moves them. On the other hand, no human being—a category to which all ballplayers and most umpires belong—is totally insensitive to other people's estimates of him, especially when the other people number in the tens of thousands. Fans can be fickle. For example, when we played the Yankees in the World Series in 1964, I faced Mickey Mantle. The first two times I struck him out. The third time he came to the plate there were scattered boos from the crowd. As luck would have it, I also struck him out that time,

This isn't to say that the fans in St. Louis are either unkind or unfeeling. A fan feels very much entitled to boo his team, or one player on that team, though he will resent it if someone who is not a staunch rooter for that team joins in the disparagement. By and large, I think Cardinal fans are fairly conservative and are quite sportsmanlike, both in their knowledge of the game and in their general courtesy.

Fans around the Country

I have neither good nor bad words for the fans at many ball parks, simply because I haven't been to some and in others I found that the crowds ranged across a predictable character spectrum. And in some ball parks I know the fans only through the baseball underground, the grapevine that carries baseball news and gossip from team to team.

A baseball stadium that is completely enclosed by grandstands may hold an uncertain peril for

---

and when Mantle walked away he was booed in a rising crescendo—this directed at one of the great players of our or any other time! The next time Mantle came to bat he was solidly booed when he approached the plate. I threw him a fast ball away—but not far enough away!—and Mantle hit it out of sight for a home run. Instantly the booing switched to cheers. Same player, same fans—just seconds apart in action and reaction. One universal feeling among ballplayers is this: They would always rather play to a crowded ball park than to an empty one. I guess this is roughly akin to the feeling that actors have about the theater *vis-à-vis* the movies: there is something uniquely stimulating about performing before a live audience, something which brings out all that you have to give.

the players, particularly if the stands are double-decked. This allows "upstairs" watchers to hurl both invective and debris upon outfielders who have aroused their ire. One such stadium is the lair of the Detroit Tigers. Another is the present (old) ball park in Philadelphia, soon to be replaced by a spanking new stadium. The fans of the Philadelphia Phillies deserve at least a line or two. They can be vicious in their baiting, and they sometimes continue to jeer at a player game after game. I do get the impression that they know their baseball, and it must also be added that they choose the targets for their attack with fine impartiality, regardless of whether he wears a Philadelphia uniform or that of a visiting ball club.

Shea Stadium is where the Mets are at home, and it is also the home of a kind of fan the sportswriters have dubbed "the New Breed." The Mets are an expansion club—meaning that when the team was formed, nine years ago, the personnel was selected from players made available from the other established teams in the league. At that time the manner in which the players were selected was such that, naturally, the better ballplayers—or what a team thought were its better ballplayers—were not available to the Mets. So the Mets had a somewhat less than glorious record for the first few years.* Somehow, the wreckage of those first few seasons fused the fans together. There are no more resolutely loyal fans anywhere than those who dote on the Mets. Shea Stadium was also the scene of the introduction of a new

* Shed no tears for the Mets. Look at where they wound up in 1969.

wrinkle in fan support: banners. These are mostly homemade, and one can see domestic cooperation in the profusion of hand-lettered sheets that adorn the ball park. There's one chap who has graduated from bedsheets to pre-printed signs. He has an extensive inventory of them, rendered in white on black for maximum visibility. When the Mets do something grand, he holds aloft a sign that says REJOICE. But if the opposition has the bases loaded and nobody out, he is likely to raise a sign that says PRAY. Banners with appropriate slogans are now present at most ball parks. But only the Mets boast a fan with an array of signs.

Not everybody can spare a sheet, but everybody can yell. At ball parks they usually do. This oral exercise has two broad categories: solo and chorus.

The chorus may be "Let's go Mets" or "Cub, Cub, Cub" (in Chicago). Or it may be the universally performed chant of "We want a hit." Sometimes, too, fans will plead for the return of a favorite player from the bench to the field. The plea is, of course, directed at the manager, who inevitably ignores it. If all this suggests to you that baseball fans are hoarse by the fifth or sixth inning, you are probably right. However, there are still other recourses available with which to signal pleasure or displeasure. One is rhythmic clapping, the steady insistence of thousands of pairs of hands beating together, yearning, pleading for a rally. Another is the waving of handkerchiefs; this only to signal furious disagreement, usually with an umpire's decision or with the appearance on the field of an opposing manager to protest a decision. If you don't have a handkerchief, you just boo, an act easily accomplished even with a hoarse voice.

It should be noted that baseball is an international pastime as well as our national one. It is played, and passionately followed by local fans, in Central and South America—notably Mexico and Venezuela—and in Puerto Rico. Perhaps the game's most devoted following overseas is in Japan, where "beisbol" is the national pastime too. But one doesn't have to travel that far to discover the multi-national appeal of baseball. The Montreal Expos are a new National League franchise and are warmly supported by their fans. Jarry Park, the home of the Expos, regularly echoes to such familiar cries as *"Nous voulons un coup sur"* ("We want a hit") and *"Tu es un vaurien"* ("You're a bum").

Entertainment at the Ball Park

Most vocalized fan activity is self-starting, but some of it is keyed by the organist. In addition to the bugler's charge—which stimulates the fans to yell, "Charge!"—there are some novel baseball fugues, as, "How Dry I Am," occasionally performed when a ballplayer goes to the water cooler. Another opus is the childhood song I can identify only through its gruesome lyrics—"The worms crawl in, the worms crawl out"—which is sometimes played as the accompaniment to a hitter who has struck out and is returning to his seat on the bench. In such instances the music will march the player back and stay with him until he actually sits down.

The organist also plays during that hallowed baseball tradition, the seventh-inning stretch. Home-team fans always stand during the minutes when the home team is leaving the field preparatory to coming to bat during the bottom of the seventh.*

Inning	1	2	3	4	5	6	7	8	9		R	H	E
Visitors	0	0	0	0	0	0	2				2	7	0
Home	1	1	0	0	0	0					2	8	1

In this drawing, the scoreboard indicates that the game is now in the bottom of the seventh inning, and therefore the home team is at bat. Notice that the board reflects the number of runs scored in each half-inning, and also totals the runs, hits, and errors for each team thus far in the game. At this point in the game the visitors have 2 runs on 7 hits and no errors, while the home team has 2 runs on 8 hits and 1 error. Of course, on a real scoreboard the names of the two competing teams would be given. But the visiting team is always on the upper horizontal line, and the home team on the lower—the top and bottom.

Now for some more comments on fans in different places. I have heard that Minnesota Twin fans are very polite; I have found San Francisco Giant fans sober (in the best sense of the word) and relatively undemonstrative. Los Angeles Dodger fans seem to spend a great deal of time watching the movie stars in the box seats, and also listen to the game on transistor radios. I don't mean this as a criticism; it's probably a good idea, but the practice is most conspicuous in Los Angeles. And let me hasten to add that whatever characterizations I've offered are purely subjective and, quite possibly, inaccurate. But

* Many fans are at first confused by the terms "top" and "bottom" of an inning. The references are drawn from the main feature of the scoreboard on which the scoring of the home team and its opponents is revealed inning by inning. It looks something like this:

they're mine, and I offer them for whatever
relevance they have, if any.

Where to Sit

Just as subjective is the question of where you
should sit in a ball park. Some people like to
sit high up, well above the field, so as to have
a panoramic view of the action. Others like to
sit behind or near first base to watch the action
there. Still others prefer the third-base and left-
field area. Some of the factors that may govern
your choice of seats are these: Do you want to
be in the sun or the shade (an irrelevant question
for night games)? Do you want to participate in
the scramble for foul balls that are lofted into
the stands? If so, the best area will be between
home and first or home and third. If you sit directly
behind home plate you will be under the "screen,"
a covering of wire, or perhaps shatter-proof glass,
that prevents pitches that are fouled off behind
the batter—like line drives going the wrong way—
from injuring the spectators.

Buying tickets for a game is inexpensive and
easy. There was a time when you could buy them
only, either in person or by mail, from the ball
park. Every club now has ticket locations in a
variety of places—banks, restaurants, sporting-
goods stores, and so forth, not only in the city
which is the namesake for the team, but in the
suburban area around each city. If you buy your
tickets by mail, be sure to indicate as clearly
as possible where you want to sit. You may not
get exactly the location you want, but the manage-
ments always try to give you at least the best
available seats. If you buy your tickets in person,
you'll probably be able to look at a seating chart

that will show more or less exactly what seats are available, and where.

The Baseball Wife as Fan

One of the reasons that I am loath to make recommendations about where to sit is that I know only one ball park really well: Busch Stadium in St. Louis, home of the Cardinals. And in truth, I do not go to as many games as you might expect—a statement that requires some explanation.

Our home is in Omaha, where Robert and I and our two daughters, Renée and Annette, live the year round. Or at least the three female Gibsons do, since of course in February, Robert reports to the Cardinal training camp in St. Petersburg, Florida. As you know, the season begins in April and lasts through September, a matter of some 6 months and 162 games. Half of those games are played on the road—that is, away from St. Louis. Which is to say that for roughly half the season Robert is not even in St. Louis, but in Pittsburgh, Cincinnati, Los Angeles, San Diego, Chicago, Houston, New York, Montreal, San Francisco, Atlanta, or Philadelphia.

Both Robert and I grew up in Omaha. We like it and its people. It is our home. Our children go to school in Omaha, and their friends are there. Early in Robert's career we had to make a decision: to move to St. Louis—and possibly elsewhere, for a ballplayer can be traded without warning from one club to another—or to remain in Omaha. We chose to remain, to keep our home and our friends, and, most important, to provide the most stable existence we could for our kids. For a time we rented a house during the season in St. Louis, but as the kids grew older it became more and more of a wrenching move for them to leave their friends during the summer.

A couple of times each year, the three Gibson girls (sorry, the sentence just typed itself) journey to St. Louis for a Cardinal "home stand"—a series of games at a team's home park—and during these periods all three of us go to the ball park. Because night games last well past little girls' bedtimes, I attend these with the wives of other players. The wives usually sit together, a seating arrangement which is clearly audible for several rows in each direction. I don't mean that we clap and shout—we do, but not with any outstanding vigor. Rather, the aural quality of our support is a kind of clanking. Over the past several years the Cardinals have won several pennants—proof of their superiority in their own (National) league —and World Series championships. For these achievements, each member of the team receives a tie tack, a watch fob, or some other small gold emblem of merit. The Cardinal wives confiscate these as quickly as they are awarded and put them on charm bracelets. They are, I suppose, the only uniform we will agree to wear. When a dozen or more of us are at a game, our applause has a distinctly metallic sound.

I do listen to a great many games on radio. When the air is free of thunderstorms and other disturbances, I can get the Cardinal games on the radio over KFEQ from St. Joseph, Missouri. Actually, I am not entirely sorry that I can't see every game Robert pitches. I watch quite a few, and I am convinced that the strain on me is far greater than that on him. I am not entirely free from superstition, so that if, for example, I have a hot dog and Robert strikes out the side—strikes out three batters in a row—I wonder if it is possible that my hot dog had something to do with it. This is an extreme case; of course diet triumphs over superstition, and Robert must fend for himself.

If I am in Omaha and Robert is either in St. Louis or on the road, he usually calls me every night. The exception is when he has pitched that afternoon or night and lost. Then he doesn't call, and since he is full of self-recrimination and self-disgust, it is perhaps just as well that he does not. That may sound selfish, or worse. I assure you it is not. Early in our marriage, and in his career, I was almost always waiting for him when he left the clubhouse. If he won, he was euphoric, though he used to review bad pitches that he had made and talk about how he would pitch to the same batter next time. If he lost . . . Well, I used to talk about everything except baseball. I'd cook one of his favorite dishes—a Creole specialty such as red beans and rice, or something really complicated, like a steak. Or I'd drag him, almost literally, to a restaurant for dinner. Nothing worked. The period following a loss was for Robert a period of despair that verged on self-hatred. Long silences would be punctuated by my chattering attempts to distract him. He would answer in monosyllables or interrupt my report on what the kids had done that day with an obviously rhetorical question: "Why didn't I keep the ball away from him?" For a while I hated all the "hims" in baseball.

Waiting for your husband outside the clubhouse door can be the prelude to a happy evening or, as I have noted, something less. And sometimes

it can be simply a very long wait. In 1968 the
Cardinals were driving toward a pennant. We
(notice the pronoun; baseball wives are confident
that our husbands' success is somehow linked to
us) had just won an important game and, since
I was in St. Louis, I joined the crowd of happy
wives waiting outside the clubhouse. Included
in the waiting group was Diane Maxvill, Cardinal
shortstop Dal Maxvill's wife. One by one our
husbands appeared, and off we went. But not
Dal. Two hours later—how long can a shower
take?—Diane found a man to go into the for-
bidden territory (NO LADIES PERMITTED BEYOND
THIS POINT) and hunt for her missing husband.
Back came the good samaritan—alone. We discovered later that Dal had completely forgotten
that Diane was waiting for him, had slipped out
a side door to elude a horde of autograph-seekers,
and had driven home—to Granite City, Illinois.
Only when he got home did he remember that he
had forgotten something: his wife. Diane has never
let him forget it, nor have the other Cardinal
wives.

Eating at the Ball Park
You may be one of those fortunate creatures who
can eat all she wants and never gain a pound
or an inch. I am not. Nonetheless, we can hardly
leave the stadium without discussing the culinary
delights that surround you. Ball-park food is
simple, wholesome, and appetizing. Food always
tastes better on a picnic than when eaten at
home. No doubt the same principle is at work
in the ball park. Or perhaps it is the excitement
of the game that stimulates the appetite, for the
sale of hot dogs has not noticeably diminished in

the Houston Astrodome. At any rate, people who go to ball parks eat, and there is a lot to choose from. If the food is obtained from luncheonette-style carry-out locations beneath the grandstands, the choice will be particularly wide: from simple sandwiches to the irresistible hot dog; and, to quench your thirst, beer, coffee, tea, beer, soda, and beer. Some ball parks also have regional or ethnic specialties. You can get a knish at Shea Stadium in New York, egg rolls in Yankee Stadium, fried chicken in Atlanta, and pizza practically everywhere. Baseball fans like to eat, a conclusion which is supported by statistics for consumption of various edibles during a year at Busch Stadium in St. Louis. As befits the beer capital of America, the stadium's refrigerators have a capacity of 264,000 bottles of beer, surely enough suds to slake the thirst of even the most dry-throated crowd at a doubleheader. To keep up with the pouring, twenty *tons* of popcorn are popped each season, and half a *million* soft pretzels are devoured. To cradle endless links of frankfurters and an army of hamburgers, one and a half million buns are devoured. To keep the fans well fed (I don't say happy; only the team on the field can do that) five hundred roving venders and two hundred stand-operators uncap and uncork, pour and dispense. And to make sure that the litter from tens of thousands of finger-lickin' repasts is removed and the stands are left pristinely clean for the next game, a broom-wielding cleaning crew of sixty-five swings into action after every game.

A ball park is a fun place to be. One thing that can make it something less than fun is being hot or cold or overdressed. Whatever the dictates of fashion may be during the season, you will certainly find the latest vogue well represented in the stands. It is neither my intention nor my right to offer opinions about the hemline struggle as personified by mini versus maxi. Given the choice, I personally would prefer to wear slacks to a ball game. This eliminates the knee-crossed sideways position you may otherwise have to assume to preserve a modicum of modesty. Pants suits—which are now popular but when you read this may have been banished to the back of the closet—combine freedom of movement for the rooter with an option of either informality or elegance.

Two factors which help make wardrobe decisions for you are the weather and the time of the game—day or night. If you are going to a game played on a warm summer afternoon, you can wear culottes—but I would vote against shorts unless you are a teen-age bride with exceptionally good legs. For a night game, though, you may want to dress up a bit. The presumption here is that you may be meeting your husband, who is coming from work. That's the reason I advance, but the real reason is, of course, that we all enjoy getting dressed up and a night game is a pretty good excuse. If you think there's something inconsistent about wearing a simple basic black—the one about which your husband said, "That much for one dress?"—and eating hot dogs in the stands you have a couple of choices. One is to have a snack before the game and a late supper afterward. At it happens, I am a sucker for the phrase "late supper." To me it conjures up a romantic idyll—flickering candles, an *intime* mood, an interlude shared by thee and he. Alas, the romance of the moment works no magic on a preoccupied pitcher intent on replaying the game pitch by pitch.

The other choice is to have dinner in the "stadium club," a separate restaurant within the stadium, reserved for fans who have season tickets. Although a few passionate (and rich) fans do have their own season tickets, for the most part such tickets are booked by corporations. Perhaps if your husband were to make a few discreet inquiries he might be able to obtain a couple of tickets with their accompanying passes to your team's stadium club. Failing that, you can have a picnic in the stands.

The Right to Second-Guess

There are many traditions which surround baseball. Most are rooted in the action on the field, in the glorious deeds of players no longer active, whose feats, surrounded by the nimbus history confers on almost all that has occurred in the past, shine with a special luminosity.

Well, fans, *we*, you and I who sit in the stands, have a hallmark of our own; a custom—nay, a passionately adhered-to ritual—which we practice, if not too wisely, then certainly too well. I refer, of course, to the second guess.

The first guess belongs to the manager. It is he, the pilot of the team, who must decide what course is to be taken. To have the batter take or hit away. To pitch to a batter or to walk him purposely. To let the pitcher stay in or bring in a relief hurler. To have the runner go or remain at first. Of such quandaries is managing made. And though it may be unfair to say that the manager has the first guess—for, as we have seen, he usually goes by the baseball book—there is, nonetheless, sufficient room for subjectivity to allow us to say that the manager's guess comes first. And *ours* is the second. What is the second guess? It is hindsight wickedly armed with generalized opinion. For example, it is the fan sitting next to you who says, after the batter has struck out and the runner from first has been thrown out, "Anybody knows Smith strikes out a lot and Jones is the slowest runner in the league, but wouldn't you know that so-and-so manager would have him running on the play?" Or, when you're a run behind and have the bases loaded with two out and the batter strikes out, "Hoky smacks, he's got three good left-handed hitters on the bench and he lets that bush-leaguer* stay in against the toughest right-hander in the league."

In other words, the second guess is an exercise in lofty managerial superiority based on an examination of what has already happened. Unfair? Yes. Fun? Delightfully so.

But—and this is a very important but—if you really want to be a mature fan, you can choose a riskier kind of guess, one that is simultaneous with that of the manager. Then and only then will you have some idea of the perilousness of managing, the nakedness of making a decision that will be proved irrevocably right or wrong before a stadium full of judges. And among those judges are you and I.

---

* The bush leagues are minor leagues. "Bush" is therefore a somewhat sneering baseball characterization, the clear implication of which is that the player or action referred to has no place in the major leagues.

The Transistorized Fan

"Hello, Weather Bureau? Can you tell me whether I'll be able to hear the Cardinal game tonight? No, they're not playing in Omaha but in St. Louis. I don't want to call the Weather Bureau in St. Louis. Anyway, the station is broadcasting from St. Joseph. And I already called them, and they said call St. Louis, and St. Louis says if I live in Omaha you should be able to tell me. I'm sorry to be a pest, but I know that if there's a storm in the area I can't get the game on the radio. . . . Do I like movies? Well, I don't have anything against them. Why? . . . It's raining in St. Louis, so I might as well go to the movies. Uh-huh. And you happen to know that *Damn Yankees* is playing in Grand Isle. Well, thanks a lot."—From the dial-twisting diary of Charline Gibson

One of the more audible phenomena of American culture is the ubiquity with which World Series broadcasts can be heard all over America. In almost any big city you can wander through a floor of an office building, ride the elevator to the lobby, take a taxi to a restaurant, and then go for a walk, and still not miss more than a pitch or two.

The World Series is a high-decibel example of the transistorized revolution in the United States, and with reason. The Series is the ultimate annual baseball drama. But the appeal of play-by-play baseball broadcasting isn't limited to the hysteria of those best-four-out-of-seven games in early fall.

Throughout the baseball season, television and radio provide a lively and vital continuity between you and your team. Each medium, in its own way, can provide a unique perspective on the game. And though neither can take the place of being at the ball park, both can make a significant contribution to the education of the baseball fan.

The Radio Broadcaster

Let us begin by considering the potential of radio to enlighten you. The medium's most obvious characteristic is that it is audio, not video. This means that the play-by-play announcer has to re-create the action on the field.

There are two challenges to the radio broadcaster. The first is the continuing play involving a long sequence of action—an inside-the-park home run, for example, in which the progress of the batter-runner circling the bases must be correlated with the efforts of the outfielders to run the ball down and relay the throw home. In other words—the broadcaster's—you must be given a simultaneous word portrait of both defensive and offensive action. Sportscasters are masters of the required techniques, able to bring you a real sense of the coinciding movements on the field.

The second challenge is at the other end of the level of action. A radio fan's interest in the game is dependent upon a flow of description, and while brief pauses are not disruptive, long periods of dead air can distort the continuity of the game, reducing the action to episodic interludes. The radio broadcaster has to pace himself, neither inundating his audience with irrelevancies nor providing a mere skeletal outline of what is happening.

One benefit that radio gives to the beginning fan is that the announcer will always set the scene. For example, if the Cardinals are trailing by a run and have two on and one out, the announcer will underline not only what the situation is but also what some of the managerial options are and why a pitch (perhaps) is particularly significant. The situation might be described thus: "The Cards are down by one. Brock leads away from second, Javier from first. Three and two on Torre at the plate. This is a big pitch, one of the turning-points in the ball game. Will the runners be going? We'll see what Red [Schoendienst, the manager] has 'em do in a minute."

Or, in another situation, rather than simply saying that Brock takes his lead, it may be: "Brock steps off from first. Now he moves off a couple of steps more. In this situation he may be going."

See? I don't mean to suggest that the same announcer's description on television won't also call attention to crucial situations, but the character of radio obviously encourages him to verbalize.

Your team's home games may be blacked out locally, but there will certainly be radio coverage. After a while you will begin to discern something less than judicial dispassion in the description, whether on radio or on the audio accompaniment to TV. This isn't a commercial attitude but a human one. Announcers are fans too. In the process of reporting their (and your) team's play, they cannot help identifying with the local heroes. This slight bias of enthusiasm on the part of broadcasters in no way detracts from their performance. On the contrary, I think it adds a humanizing note. After all, baseball is an emotional game, and fans quite naturally appreciate the special interest their announcers have in their team.

Play-by-play announcers vary enormously in microphone personality, in announcing style. Some underplay what is happening; others dramatize the events. If the announcer is a former ballplayer, he will issue praise or criticism consonant with his own experience in the game. Consciously or otherwise, most announcers have developed their own patented descriptions of a home run. Harry Caray, who together with Jack Buck broadcast the Cardinal games for years, had a home-run description that was guaranteed to keep you aquiver with expectancy. "There's a long drive. It may be." (Pause.) "It could be." (Pause.) "It is!" Oh, those pauses of uncertainty!

Jack Buck tells me that there is a headset in the Cardinal dugout which he uses during pregame shows when the team is playing at home. Occasionally the ballplayers listen to the broadcast of the game as it is aired, and they often tease the broadcasters about their descriptions when the game is over. Jack also says that while the players—of the opposing teams, as well as the Cardinals—do not take offense at some of the harsher realities of play-by-play ("Gibson had a play at second but didn't see it," or, "So-and-so took his eye off the ball, he should have made the catch") the players' wives are far less tolerant.

I suppose that says something about the female of the species, and perhaps explains why there aren't any female sportscasters.

Many broadcasters have been describing their teams' games on the air for years. It isn't too surprising that they feel a special kinship with the teams. Most broadcasters ride the team bus from hotel to ball park when the team is on the road, and in a variety of ways tend to become a part of the team's "official family." They often conduct pre-game and post-game shows on radio and television. Naturally these shows are built around interviews with ballplayers. One result of this is that the fans begin to see (and hear) ballplayers as people and not merely as uniforms with numbers.

The Television Broadcaster

When he is providing the play-by-play description for television, the announcer's role is subtly different. He must avoid the redundancy of articulating what is clearly visible on the screen. He must add to the image, not create it as is done on radio.

The benefit of watching baseball on television is, of course, that you see the action. On a close play or a particularly satisfying one—your guys making a fine play in the field or hitting a homer—you may even see it several times. I refer to the wizardry of video tape, which allows you to see the action and savor the moment again. Interestingly, when video-taping and the consequent replay of the action first gained acceptance, many people in baseball wondered about its effect on the accuracy of umpires' rulings. The fans,

I suspect, didn't wonder; they were sure that on replay everyone would see that the umpire was wrong and their team had been victimized by an unjust decision. Nothing of the kind has happened. On the contrary, video tape has proven that the umpires are not only more often right than wrong, but right in the very great majority of cases.

Given this electronic capability, you might think —as I did—that perhaps the day of the live umpire was drawing to a close. After all, why not have electronic eyes call balls and strikes and "see" every play on tape before rendering a computerized decision? I put this question to Commissioner Bowie Kuhn. His answer was that to surrender the decision-making responsibility of an umpire to a machine would be to deprive baseball of its humanness. Just, he said, as pressure in a crucial game situation will bring out the best in some players and cause others to perform below par, or as managers may err in their decisions, so the umpire contributes a human dimension— of judgment—to the intensely human game of baseball. On reflection, I must admit I think the Commissioner is right.

Back to baseball on television. During the season, NBC broadcasts its Game of the Week on Saturday afternoons, and occasionally a night game during the week. The Game of the Week is generally broadcast from a different stadium every week, so you have an opportunity to see teams in both leagues and from distant cities. In addition to the geographical variety, NBC has pioneered a number of innovations in televised baseball. It was the first to use video tape to play back crucial action, and the first to broadcast baseball games in color. The Game of the Week also introduced a split-screen, isolated-camera technique which helps compensate for the fact that, though we have two eyes, we can follow only a single action at a time.

Here's how the technique works. Suppose the situation is such as to suggest that the hit-and-run may be on. Well then, on the left side of your screen one camera will focus on the batter, and on the right side of the screen another camera will follow the movement of the runner at first. The announcer's voice will cue the action: So-and-so "goes to the rubber, sets—and the pitch . . ." Your ears tell you what the pitcher is doing; your eyes tell you whether the runner is or isn't going, whether the batter is hitting or taking.

Yet another NBC Game of the Week feature is slow-motion replay. This enables you not only to see a home run again but also to observe the flowing power of a batter's swing as it progresses from stance at the plate to follow-through. The same technique applied to a tumbling catch underlines the acrobatic ability of the outfielder, his grace, his hustle.

Most baseball games are televised with three cameras. One is behind home plate, giving an over-the-shoulder view of umpire, catcher, batter, and pitcher. This view is one of the best ways of proving to yourself that a breaking ball really does break. Another camera is behind first base, and another is behind third base. These cameras can sweep the field, coming in close for some shots, panning other action if that is required. Sometimes a fourth camera is mounted in center field. This enables the viewer to "be" on the mound with the pitcher, to see the threatening pose of the hitter just as he does, and to take the sign from the catcher.

Jack Buck reminds me that most fans do not appreciate the coordination between audio and video that is required to provide good television coverage of a ball game. One of the keys to such coordinated coverage is the director. All the TV cameras are "on" at all times, and it is the director who determines, along with the announcer, which of the several pictures available you will see. So the director and his cameramen must be as prescient visually as the announcers are orally.

The limitation of television is that the screen is limited, and cameras cannot focus as swiftly as your eyes. When you watch someone run out a triple on television, you miss the correlation of the runner churning round the bases, and the outfielder pursuing the ball. You will, or may, see the runner and ball arrive simultaneously at third base, but your eye gets there abruptly, not smoothly and logically. On an infield play you will see the third baseman make a great play, stop, and begin his throw, but the next thing you see is the ball arriving at first base. You lose the dimension of depth and of distance, as though the start of the play at third and its conclusion at first are mismatched halves of two different actions.

At least that's my opinion. Which isn't to say that I don't enjoy watching baseball on television, or listening to the game on radio. I do, despite the fact that the game is narrowed in the sense that the action is squeezed onto a screen or into the articulated point of view of the sportscaster. Nonetheless, you can't get to every ball game and,

as I said, I do think that at this stage of the game—
our game, that is—you can learn a great deal from
the men behind the microphones.

But there is only one place, really, to learn
about baseball, to see what it is that makes fans
hoarse from shouting, to taste the excitement in
the air, to see all the action, all the color. That
place is the ball park.

And it's our place, too.

Appendix

Keeping Score

Baseball records are the bench marks against which a player can be compared with his peers today, or even with the storied heroes of the past. In a very real sense, the official scorer's notations are the yesterdays of baseball, for only through them can we check on what really happened in a game, an inning, an at-bat.

In a much more personal way you can, and should, keep score whenever you go to a game. (I do know a number of baseball wives who keep score at home while listening to or watching a game, and perhaps eventually you will too. But at least in the beginning, I suggest you score a game at the ball park.) For one thing, only real fans keep score. For another, it will impress the heck out of your husband—and, most especially, the kids.

For no more than a quarter, you can get the day's official program and scorecard. Another nickel or so will get you a pencil. (A word of caution about the pencils: always bring your own; the ones sold in the ball park are either sharpened to such a fine point that they break instantly, or so dull that the lead vanishes after three or four innings.) If you open your program to the center fold, you will discover a series of ruled boxes occupying both pages. The left-hand page is for the visiting club; the right-hand page is for the home team. In the margins, the pages list the rosters of both teams, always giving you the uniform number of the player, his last name, and his position.

Directly under the name of each team is a series of vertical blanks. This is where you list the lineups for each team as announced over the public-address system. There are more than nine spaces because (sob) the starting pitcher may have to be relieved, or a pinch-hitter or pinch-runner may be required. Once you have entered the lineups, you are ready to keep score—baseball's shorthand. I suggest you begin with the traditional one, a sort of baseball Gregg.

Every position is given a number:

> 1—pitcher
> 2—catcher
> 3—first baseman
> 4—second baseman
> 5—third baseman
> 6—shortstop
> 7—left fielder
> 8—center fielder
> 9—right fielder

The numbers replace positions in scoring. Note that the numbers are used *only* to indicate defensive play. A single number shows that a player has flied out, two numbers indicate that a player has grounded out, and three numbers that a player has hit into a double play. Thus you will often hear a broadcaster say that so-and-oo "hit into a six-four-three double play"—a double play started by the shortstop, who flipped to the second baseman, who threw on to the first baseman.

The performance of the leadoff batter is entered in the first box under inning number one. Let's say he grounds out short to first. In that box you put: 6-3. The second player flies to right. Enter a 9 in his box. The third man up strikes out. Enter a K, the universal symbol for a strikeout, in his box. Now switch pages in the scorebook because the home team is up. You will return to the first page when the visiting team comes up in the second inning, placing your annotations in the second vertical column.

Scoring a baseball game is easy until someone gets on base. Then you need a sharp pencil and a steady hand.

Consider each box a miniature diagram of a baseball diamond, with home plate in the lower left-hand corner. Chart the progress of the batter-runner counterclockwise, with first base in the lower right-hand corner. What you do is follow his progress on the bases and indicate how he got there.

Here are the standard symbols:

Single	—	Reached base on error	E
Double	=	Fielder's choice	FC
Triple	≡	Hit by pitch	HP
Home run	≣	Wild pitch	WP
Stolen base	B	Struck out	K
Sacrifice fly	SF	Base on balls	BB
Sacrifice bunt	SB	Force-out	FO
Passed ball	PB		
Balk	BK		

Here is a single box diagramed to show the following. The batter reached first on an error by the shortstop, stole second, went to third on a wild pitch, and scored on a passed ball. To show that a run scored on a certain play, draw a circle around that play, as indicated:

Each of the two pages in the program used for scoring has places in which you can total the runs, hits, and errors for the game. At the end of the game you will have bitten the end of your pencil instead of your nails, and your scorebook will be crowded with the scratched notations that make baseball history. You can take the program home, and a year later, or five years later, or thirty years later, you can read back the players who tried, failed, were there, and tell which ones did what and which ones didn't.

So be a baseball historian, and know the score.

Glossary

The language of baseball may occasionally seem to be as mysterious to you as the game once was. But, as with any language, fluency comes from use, and understanding matures from literal definition to easy familiarity.

Like any language, that of baseball is constantly being enriched by new words. New idioms are added, and conversely, expressions that were once relied upon by player, sportswriter, and fan are now simply anachronistic anagrams. "Foozle," I have been told by a wizened baseball expert, once meant to bungle a play, to commit an error. The same white-haired consultant informs me that "Dexter meadow" was a synonym for right field. Who was Dexter, some famous outfielder of bygone times? Or not a person but a place? I don't know.

The same baseball ancient tells me that "to peddle Peruna" meant to engage in boastful talk. Who was (or is) Peruna? Did he have a first name—or is Peruna a place, perhaps a ball park in some ghostly minor-league town, the outfield walls warped and askew, the infield choked with weeds, the turnstiles rusty and silent?

Again, I have no answers. But you will—in the contemporary language of today's game. This is not to say that what appears hereafter is either unabridged or Webster-like in its unquestionable authority. But you will be able to understand what may have previously seemed incoherent and, armed with a working vocabulary, be able to join in the greatest of American debates.

Aboard—Said of a runner when he is on base.

Ace—The best pitcher on any team's staff.

American League—One of the two major leagues, sometimes called the junior circuit because it is the younger (the other being the National League.) The American League includes twelve teams divided into two six-team divisions. The American League Eastern Division includes the Baltimore Orioles, Boston Red Sox, Cleveland Indians, Detroit Tigers, New York Yankees, and Washington Senators.

The American League Western Division includes the California Angels, Chicago White Sox, Kansas City Royals, Minnesota Twins, Oakland Athletics, and Seattle Pilots.

At the end of the season, the teams that finish first—achieve the best won-lost records—in both divisions engage in a best-three-out-of-five-game playoff. The winner of this "mini-Series" wins the American League pennant and the right to represent the American League in the World Series against the National League pennant-winner.

Appeal play—Act of a fielder claiming violation of the rules by the offensive team.

Apple—A baseball.

Assist—A throw or deflection of a batted ball that contributes to a putout.

Automatic strike—The pitch thrown when the count is three balls, no strikes. There's nothing automatic about it, merely that in many cases the batter will be taking and the pitcher can lay the ball in.

Bag—Common name for any base except home. Other synonyms are "sack" and "cushion." The terms

"two-bagger," "three-bagger," and "four-bagger" refer, respectively, to a double, a triple, and a home
run.

Balk—An illegal act—often the failure to complete a
pick-off throw by the pitcher with his foot on the
rubber—committed by a pitcher with runners on
base which allows each runner to advance one base.

Baltimore chop—A ball hit down on the infield, usually
toward third, which takes a high bounce, compelling
the fielder to wait for it.

Bases loaded—A runner at each base. Baseball announcers often spin their own expressions, based
on the home city, as FOB, full of Braves (Atlanta)
or Birds (St. Louis Cardinals, Baltimore Orioles).
Synonyms often heard are: "They're loaded up,"
"They're jammed," "They're crammed."

Batting average—Often called a percentage, but in
actuality a fraction arrived at by dividing the hits
a batter has made by his total of official at-bats—
that is, excluding walks, sacrifices, being hit by a
pitched ball, but including the times the batter
reached base on an error.

Beanball—A ball pitched at a batter's head with the
intention of driving him back from the plate. A
batter hit by such a pitch is referred to as having
been beaned.

Blank—To pitch one inning or more without per-
mitting a run.

Bleachers—The least expensive seats, usually in center
field, and frequently unroofed.

Blooper—A softly hit ball that falls safely in the outfield for a hit, just beyond the reaching fingers of
several pursuing players. A ball so hit has been
blooped.

Bobble—To fail to handle a ground ball cleanly. Not
necessarily an error, though: "Smith bobbles the
ground ball, throws just in time for the out."

Bunch—To group hits together so as to maximize their
potential to produce runs.

Called game—One in which, for any reason, the umpire-in-chief terminates play before the game has been completed.

Cellar—Last place in the standings. Also referred to as the basement.

Chinese homer—A less than mighty blow that sneaks into the stands barely fair for a home run. The term is gradually falling into disuse as new ball parks are built which conform to minimum foul-line specifications of 325 feet, as opposed to a previous minimum of 250 feet.

Circus catch—An outstanding catch in the field, often of acrobatic quality.

Choke—To hold the bat well up on its handle. Also, to panic in any difficult situation.

Circuit clout—A home run.

Clothesline—A hit, usually a single, that travels "straight as a clothesline." Also referred to as "a frozen rope."

Clutch—A time of crisis in the game. Thus a clutch hitter is one whom fortune favors with key hits during crucial portions of the game. "Good in the clutch" is a favorite baseball encomium. A pitcher can be good in the clutch, but he is usually referred to as "having it in the clutch." None of this has anything to do with what your husband means when he says, "Don't ride the clutch."

Crowding the plate—Standing as close to home plate as the boundaries of the batter's box allow. Hitters who crowd the plate often get hit by "legitimate" inside pitches.

Dead ball—A ball that is not "live" because play has been suspended by the umpire, or automatically—as in the case of a line drive bouncing into the stands and being subject to the ground rules.

DP—A double play.

Drag bunt—A bunt characterized by the batter beginning to run to first simultaneously with the bunt itself. Drag bunts are almost always up the first-base line and are almost certainly bunts for a base hit, as opposed to sacrifice bunts.

Duster—A pitch that dumps the batter on his dignity in the dust around the batter's box.

Earned-Run Average—Always expressed as ERA, this represents the legitimate number of earned runs— that is, runs scored as the result of hits, without benefit of errors—that a pitcher gives up during an average nine innings. A pitcher's ERA is computed by dividing the number of innings pitched into the total number of earned runs allowed. The resultant figure is carried to two decimal points—as 2.73, meaning that the pitcher in question has given up an average of 2.73 runs per nine innings. An ERA of 3.00 is good. One lower than that is excellent.

Fan—As a noun, the word refers to the genus *baseball enthusiasticus*. As a verb, it means to strike out. "Bob Gibson fans" means that Bob Gibson has struck out. "Bob Gibson fanned eight" means that as a pitcher RG has retired eight batters by striking them out.

Fielder's choice—The decision of a fielder when making a play on a batted ball to retire a runner rather than the batter. If Gibson hits a ground ball to short with Maxvill on second, and Dal tries to go to third, the shortstop will throw to the third baseman, who will put the tag on Maxvill. Gibson is safe at first on the fielder's choice. (And Dal, you should know better than to try and move from second to third on a ground ball hit ahead of you.)

Foul tip—A batted ball that goes sharply and directly from the bat to the catcher's hands and is legally caught. It is not a foul tip unless caught, and any such foul that is caught is a strike, and the ball is in play. It is not a catch if it is a rebound, unless the ball has first touched the catcher's glove or hand.

Frame—An inning.

Full count—Three strikes and two balls on the batter.

Gopher ball—A pitch that is hit for a home run.

Grand slam—A home run with the bases loaded.

Grapefruit league—Informal spring-training league in Florida.

Ground rules—Special rules pertaining to the particular stadium in which a game is being played. For example, here are the ground rules for Busch Stadium:

Outfield Area: Fair ball hitting above yellow line in left and right fields—HOME RUN. Ball hitting on or below yellow line is IN PLAY. Fair ball bounding into field boxes, bleachers, garden area in center field, or enclosed area in left- or right-field corners—TWO BASES.

Dugouts: Ball rolling onto top step (at ground level) of either dugout is IN PLAY. Photographers' area on outfield end of each dugout shall be regarded as part of the dugout. Ball thrown by pitcher from the rubber to catch baserunner off first or third base that goes into stand or dugout—ONE BASE. A pitched, thrown, or batted ball that hits anyone on the playing field except as otherwise provided for in the Official Playing Rules is IN PLAY. Any batted ball hitting automatic tarpaulin container would be a FOUL BALL. Ball going through wire behind plate or lodging in it—ONE BASE on throw by pitcher, TWO BASES on throw by fielder.

Hill—The pitcher's mound.

Horsehide—A baseball.

Hot corner—Third base.

Hurler—A pitcher.

Infield hit—A base hit which does not get through the infield. A bunt single, of course, but also a smash deep in the hole (any hole) or a ball knocked down in desperation, but on which no play—that is, no throw—can be made.

Issue a pass—To give a base on balls.

Jam—As a noun, a tight spot that a pitcher and his team may find themselves in (for instance, bases loaded and nobody out). As a verb, the action of a pitcher in throwing inside in such a fashion that the batter hits the ball off the handle of the bat—i.e., weakly.

Jug-handled curve—A big, wide-breaking curve ball.

Keystone bag—Second base.

Keystone combination—Shortstop and second baseman.

Kick the game away—To lose a game because of errors in the field or mental lapses.

Knot the count—A phrase which is slowly receding into history. It can mean to tie the score of a game, or to even up that ball-and-strike count.

Knocked out of the box—Said of a pitcher removed for allowing too many hits and/or runs. Variations on this most unhappy theme include: "sent to the showers," "taking an early shower," "getting shelled."

Leadoff man—The first batter up in the game, that is, the batter in the number-one position in the batting order. Or the first batter up in an inning.

Left stranded—Said of a runner left on base (who has, therefore, missed the opportunity to score).

Lift a pitcher—To replace a pitcher, usually because he has been knocked out of the box.

Liner—A line drive.

Load the sacks—Load the bases.

LOB—Left on base, runners left stranded. A high figure—11 LOB—means a team is not capitalizing on its scoring opportunities.

Loop—A baseball league.

Lumber—A baseball bat.

Mound duel—A baseball game that is largely a contest between two overpowering pitchers.

Nail a runner—Throw a runner out on a close play, usually said of a runner trying to steal or to score.

National League—One of the two major leagues, sometimes called the Senior Circuit because it is the older (the other being the American League). The National League includes twelve teams divided into two six-team divisions. The National League Eastern Division includes the Chicago Cubs, Montreal Expos, New York Mets, Philadelphia Phillies, Pittsburgh Pirates, and St. Louis Cardinals.

The National League Western Division includes the Atlanta Braves, Cincinnati Reds, Houston Astros, Los Angeles Dodgers, San Diego Padres, and San Francisco Giants.

At the end of the season the teams that finish first—achieve the best won-lost records—in both divisions engage in a best-three-out-of-five-game play-off. The winner of this "mini-Series" wins the National League pennant and the right to represent the National League in the World Series against the American League pennant-winner.

Nick—To get a minimum number of hits and runs. A pitcher gets *nicked* for one run and two hits in an inning. More than that, and the verbs and adjectives slice more deeply into hyperbole.

Nightcap—The second game of a doubleheader.

No-hitter—A game in which a pitcher does not give up so much as one hit. Not necessarily a shutout, though.

Obstruction—The act of a fielder who, while not in possession of the ball and not in the act of fielding the ball, impedes the progress of any runner.

On deck—The situation of the batter who will be up after the one now at the plate. Of the three men who are guaranteed to be up in an inning, the first batter is at the plate; the second is on deck; the third is in the hole.

One away—One out.

Pass—A base on balls; an intentional pass is a purposely issued base on balls.

Passed ball—A pitch that goes past the catcher, allowing a runner to advance, which, in the judgment of the official scorer, the catcher should have been able to handle.

Pay-off pitch—The pitch thrown when the count is full, three balls and two strikes.

Pea—A baseball.

Peg—A throw.

Pellet—A baseball.

Perfect game—A no-hitter in which the pitcher faces and retires twenty-seven men in nine innings.

Pickoff—A throw by a pitcher or a catcher to a fielder in an attempt to catch a runner off base.

Pill—A baseball.

Pilot—A manager of a baseball team.

Pinch-hitter—A batter substituted for one originally supposed to be up at that time.

Pinch-runner—A replacement for a baserunner.

Pine-tar rag—A rag blackened with pine tar that batters apply either to the handles of their bats or, somewhat more gingerly, to their hands. In either case, the idea is to overcome the combination of smooth wood and human perspiration which can make for slippery hitting.

Pitchout—A pitch deliberately thrown wide of the plate so that the catcher is in a better position to throw out a runner attempting to steal.

Platter—Home plate, which is also referred to as "the dish."

"Play"—The umpire's order to start the game or to resume action following any dead ball.

Play over his head—To perform better than expected.

Pop fly—A ball hit no great distance horizontally, though perhaps quite high, and, unless otherwise specified, not a hit. Exception: a pop-fly double, for example, is a pop fly that no fielder can get to, so that the ball falls in fair ground for a double.

Pop-fly foul—A pop fly hit into foul ground.

Pop-up—A pop fly.

Pop—Verbal form of "pop fly" and the last such, I promise. "He pops the ball up" means the batter has hit a pop fly. (Yes, I know it really should be listed earlier in the glossary, but it's easier to understand if you have read the other POPular definitions first.)

Pull hitter—A hitter who normally hits "ahead" of the ball: a left-handed batter who normally hits the

ball to right field, a right-handed batter who normally hits the ball to left field.

Pull the string—To throw a slow pitch after a series
of fast balls. Also a synonym for throwing a change-
of-pace.

Rally—A combination of hits, walks, or the opponents'
errors which produces one or more runs. "Rally" has
the distinct connotation of catching up. You rally
to knot the score—to achieve a tie—or to go ahead.

Rap—As a verb, almost exclusively applied to ground
balls. "Rapped into a double play," for example.

Reach—An interesting baseball verb that is found in
some rather dissimilar expressions: "He reached on
a walk in the second" means that the batter in
question was walked in the second inning; "Gibson
reached back for something extra" means that
Gibson tapped his reserves of strength to throw
particularly hard—and note that only pitchers reach
back for something extra, never hitters; "They
reached Gibson for a run in the sixth" means that
the opposition (finally) scored a run in the sixth
inning.

Resin bag—A bag of powdered resin is kept on the
pitcher's mound. When a pitcher "goes to the resin
bag" he is dusting his hands and fingertips with
resin to get a better grip on the ball. Batters have a
resin bag to help them get a better grip on the
handle of the bat.

Rhubarb—An argument on the baseball field, often
turbulent and most certainly impassioned.

Ride the bench—To sit on the bench and, therefore,
not play.

Rip—One of an honored collection of verbs im-
mortalized by sportswriters in an attempt to convey
the mind-expanding sight and sound of a solidly
hit ball. A grounder can be ripped, so the word
isn't limited to line drives, but it is usually applied
to them. "Rip" may be an abbreviation of "rip the

cover off the ball"—but that's just a guess. Other hard-hitting verbs are: "smack," "smash," "power," "rocket," "wallop," "crash," "cream," and "blast."

Rock—A boner, as often as not mental rather than an error of play. A rock is a dumb play or a missed play.

Roundhouse curve—A big, slow curve, big in the sense that it breaks significantly.

Round the horn—A double play which is started by the third baseman, who throws to either the shortstop or second baseman covering the keystone sack, who in turn throws on to the first baseman.

Round-tripper—A home run.

Rubber-armed—Said of a pitcher who can hurl frequently and for a considerable number of innings without suffering soreness in his shoulder or arm.

Rub up the ball—To remove some of the glossiness from the ball. Either a pitcher or catcher (or both) may briskly rub the ball between his hands when a new ball is put in play.

RBI—Run batted in. A batter gets credit for an RBI when he bats in a run with a hit (including his own run if he gets a homer), an infield out, a sacrifice fly, or a bunt, or when he gets a walk with the bases loaded.

Rundown—The chase when a runner is trapped off base, in which the ball is tossed back and forth between two or more fielders as they try to tag the runner before he can get safely back to a base. A baserunner in this situation is being run down, and the fielders are running him down. A rundown is sometimes called a pickle.

Sack—A base. Derivatives include first-, second-, and third-sacker; that is, first baseman, second baseman, third baseman.

Sacrifice fly—A fly ball, either fair or foul, which is long enough to allow a baserunner to tag up and score.

Scattered hits—No more than one hit per inning: a pitcher who allows only scattered hits effectively denies the offense an opportunity to score. (Opposite of bunched hits.)

Shagging flies—Outfield practice at catching fungoes before the game begins.

Shake-off—Negative motion of pitcher's head, indicating to the catcher that the pitcher does not want to throw the pitch for which the catcher has signaled.

Shoestring catch—A catch by an outfielder of a ball at shoe level—that is, right above the grass. Usually occurs after a long run by the outfielder.

Shutout—Game in which one team does not score.

Skipper—The manager, also called the pilot, or MGR.

Slugging average—A measure of a batter's power, as found by dividing his at-bats into his total bases. The latter is the sum of his hits and bases: one for each single, two for each double, three for each triple, four for each homer. Example: if a batter has been up 100 times and has 30 hits (20 singles, 5 doubles, 4 triples, 1 home run), his total bases are 30 (hits) plus 10 (5 two-base hits) plus 12 (4 three-base hits) plus 4 (1 four-base hit), for a total base sum of 56. Divided by 100, that gives a slugging average of .560. If a batter hit a home run every time he came to bat, his slugging average would be 5.00. Wow!

Slump—For a batter, a period during which he does not get any, or many, hits; the batter is *in* a slump, and his batting average slumps. For a team, a slump is a losing streak.

Spray—To hit to all fields.

Strand—To leave runners on base at the end of an inning.

Swinging bunt—Play in which the batter takes a full swing but only taps the ball, achieving the effect of a bunt. A swinging bunt is an accident, but one that usually gets the batter to first base with a hit.

Suspended game—A called game which is to be completed at a later date. (See Called game.)

Tally—A run; also, to score a run.

Tee off—To swing lustily. Usually used in a situation in which the hitters have been hitting long drives; that is, they've not only been swinging hard but also connecting.

Texas-leaguer—A weakly hit fly or "softly" hit line drive that falls between inrushing outfielders and outrushing infielders. It also can be used in a slightly belittling sense, in that balls hit that way are okay in the Texas League (a minor league), but not up here in the majors.

Thumbed (out)—Ejected from the game by an umpire.

"Time"—The announcement by an umpire of a legal interruption of play, during which the ball is dead. (See Play.) "Time" is also what the batter requests from the umpire when he steps out of the batter's box. In theory, the umpire can deny the batter's request, but in practice, permission is always granted.

Toil—To pitch.

Tomato—A baseball.

Trickles—Said of a baseball that meanders slowly down the first- or third-base line.

Twin bill—A doubleheader.

Twi-nighter—A doubleheader with the first game beginning in the late afternoon, normally around five o'clock.

Triple Crown—Distinction of a batter who, when the season ends, leads his league in batting average, home runs, and RBIs.

Walk—A base on balls.

Waste a pitch—To throw a pitch deliberately out of the strike zone as when the pitcher is out in front with a count of 0 and 2. Also referred to as "wasting one."

Whiff—To swing and miss. Also, to strike someone out, as in "Gibson whiffed two [batters] in the seven innings he pitched."

Wild—Said of a pitcher who has lost his control. A pitcher who is just missing the corners is generally not referred to in this way.

Wild pitch—A pitch that is too wide, high, or low for the catcher to handle, and which allows a runner to advance.